THE
INTERCESSIONS
HANDBOOK

Also by John Pritchard:

Beginning Again (SPCK 2000)

(with Paul Ballard)
Practical Theology in Action (SPCK 1996)

THE INTERCESSIONS HANDBOOK

Creative ideas for public and private prayer

JOHN PRITCHARD

First published in Great Britain 1997
Society for Promoting Christian Knowledge
Holy Trinity Church
Marylebone Road
London
NW1 4DU

Fourth impression 2001

British Library Cataloguing in Publication Data

A catalogue record for this book is available from the
British Library

ISBN 0-281-04979-3

Typeset by Pioneer Associates Ltd, Perthshire
Printed in Great Britain by
J. W. Arrowsmith Ltd, Bristol

CONTENTS

FOREWORD

In his own ministry Jesus spoke about the importance of intercession on many occasions. Whether one thinks of the Sermon on the Mount, his parables or his private talks with his disciples, encouragements to them to learn to intercede are never far away. Yet so often the ministry of intercession is neglected both in our personal lives and in those of our Churches. Sometimes we may feel that a particular need is too trivial to bring to God – at others we are overwhelmed by the enormity of a situation and do not know where to begin to focus our prayers. Likewise in our public intercessions it is easy to become banal, or to drift into a 'shopping list' approach that allows no time for the congregation to concentrate on the different areas of need.

John Pritchard is well aware of these and many other pitfalls and at the same time is fully committed to the importance of intercession. He rightly describes this as a handbook – one to be referred to time and again whether we are seeking to develop our private intercessions, or thinking how we can lead them still better in a small group or at public worship.

It is a book which I hope will be widely used in the coming years as we learn afresh to intercede both for ourselves and for others and I warmly commend it to you.

✠ George Cantuar
ARCHBISHOP OF CANTERBURY

1 THE CHALLENGE OF INTERCESSION

'Let us pray for the Church and for the world, and let us thank God for a short sleep.' That at least is how it seems when on a Sunday morning someone begins to lead the intercessions. We have had the readings, which were fine except for some confusion about why we had the bit from Judges about Jael driving a tent-peg through Sisera's temple. Then we had the sermon, which took us on a breathless tour from the Garden of Eden to the Gates of Paradise in twelve minutes. We cantered briefly through the enormous statements of the Creed, and now we have reached the relative calm of the intercessions.

Here at least we know where we are: a few minutes of well-meaning prayer, listing most of the people and places we brought to God's attention last week. It may not do any harm, but the problem really is simply to stay with it after the first few phrases. After all, the eyes are closed – legitimately – and no one can see that we have nodded off, or our mind has wandered to that patch of rust we noticed this morning by the rear bumper.

Suddenly the intercessions are over, or at least we seem to have gone on to a prayer that everyone is saying, so they must be over. And so one of the high points of the service has passed again, the time when the people of God join together to intercede on behalf of the whole world. This is an enormous privilege and responsibility. We have the awesome task of holding open to the Father those parts of his creation which stand in need of renewal. Here great issues of Church, politics, and human destiny are being hammered out. Or, to lower the stakes a bit, here people's health and well-being are being restored or maintained. This isn't a task for the faint-hearted.

Unfortunately this is not generally the way that the prayers of intercession in church worship are understood. The impact they make is more akin to being savaged by a feather duster. Why is this?

SOME COMMON PROBLEMS

Generality So often the prayers are couched in such vast categories that they seem to mean something and nothing. I remember kneeling in the chapel of St George's Windsor, and being told we were praying that morning for the Indian Ocean. What in particular, I wondered? The algae, perhaps, or a revival in medium-sized waves? Prayers which are left at the level of 'And now we pray for China', leave God with a great deal of manoeuvrability. They also leave the congregation floundering. What aspect of China? Its life, leadership, human rights record, relations with the West, Hong Kong, the Church, evangelism, theological education? Where do you break into such a vast task as praying for China? Without particularity, prayers of intercession can be frustrating and meaningless for the congregation. We have to trust that God is more adept at using our prayers than we are at thinking them through.

Repetition Sometimes you can feel that last week's script of prayers has just been handed over wholesale to this week's leader. Did we not pray for exactly those same church leaders in exactly the same way? Is not that list of the sick just the same, and just as uninformative as last week's? Was that a rogue troublespot which crept into this week's list, or was it perhaps the turbulent product of a fevered expectation? We have a stern biblical warning about vain repetition. We might protest that our repetition is not at all vain but is the regular holding of needs before the Lord of heaven. But if corporate prayer is intended to lead the people of God in their joint, committed intercession, then those people have to be kept awake; their persistence in prayer has to be won by thoughtful, imaginative leading of the time of intercession.

Dullness Much public prayer lacks a sense of the vitality and colour of the world for which we are praying. All too easily it can be a mild person speaking to a mild God in a mild way on behalf of a mild congregation, hoping, presumably, that God will not answer these prayers too energetically! The final insult and indignity to Christian faith is to reduce it to anaemic and hesitant ramblings about being nice to each other. We are dealing with ultimate issues of life and death in a faith that should terrify and excite us, attract us and render us speechless. Here is a faith of enormous intellectual and emotional range, and a God, the riches of whose character are beyond our wildest imaginings. Surely prayer to such a God should not be boring! And if we are leading prayers in worship it should take all our ingenuity, determination and creativity to try and do justice to such a mighty task.

Disbelief When we pray in church on a Sunday morning it should not be necessary to believe six impossible things before coffee! If I am expected to subscribe to a prayer which asks God to prevent all accidents on the road this Bank Holiday weekend, I am being set an intellectual and spiritual conundrum. If I am a nurse and I hear simplistic prayers that so-and-so will be physically healed when I know full well that under normal conditions so-and-so has terminal cancer, then I am being asked to leave my mind at home. My prayers will not want to exclude different forms of healing, but they will want to be more nuanced. The fact is that we are all working with our own theologies, and the range of different views in the average congregation, from red-blooded orthodoxy to enquiring agnosticism, demands real care in our use of words and ideas. This should not have the effect of reducing every prayer to bland politeness, but it should give pause to our sloppy thinking as we put prayers together.

What I have suggested above is a range of problems with intercession in public worship. But that is not all! Prayers in all-age worship present another set of issues. Can you avoid 'bunny rabbit' prayers which put Jesus on a level with a furry friend you grew out of when you were eight? Can you avoid making Jesus sound like a bigger and sleeker version of Superman who solves personal and

3

international crises as effortlessly as he rips off his shirt and tie? How can prayer be relevant, vivid and varied, and yet introduce people to the riches of long traditions of Christian prayer which will help them to grow? How can you involve small children in the same act of prayer as adults? These are not superficial questions of technique; they require prolonged reflection to ensure that what is offered in prayer has a solid basis in our understanding of faith development, spirituality and theology.

The quest for good intercessions gets stickier still when we think of prayer in small groups, such as abound in church life today. Is there not a paucity of imagination in the ways many groups pray? The period of open prayer with which most house groups probably close their formal session is an excellent and powerful witness to the faith, love and persistence of thousands of Christian people. But the message which is often reinforced by such times of prayer is that this is the only valid way of bringing needs to God in group settings, and if you find this hard, embarrassing or just plain boring, you will have to remain a second-class pray-er. Surely there are other ways of making prayer in small groups vivid and engaging? Might not our enthusiasm for intercession be revived and stimulated by exploring other ways of doing it?

The bedrock of intercessory prayer is the disciplined or spontaneous, faithful or fanciful daily prayer of individual Christians. Here at last is the safe haven of personal prayer. Unfortunately all is not as well as it seems. There is an inner hesitancy in the heart of many Christians when it comes to intercession. It comes in two forms.

First there is often a nagging feeling that intercession is a chore. Do I really have to go through all these people again? Could they not get on just as well without my prayers today? Indeed (I might think rather dangerously), might they not have a rather more exciting time if I let them off the leash of my prayers every so often? No, all right then – here we go again . . .

Sometimes prayer is spectacular and urgent. Dean Inge once received an angry letter from a lady who disagreed with an article he had written. 'I am praying night and day for your death,' she wrote. 'It may interest you to know that in two other cases I was successful.' Such prayer was doubtless lively and committed, even if entirely erroneous and unanswered. Nevertheless much ordinary intercession is simply bread and butter prayer for much less exciting projects. And it can easily become a chore.

The second form of hesitancy felt by many Christians about regular intercession is that such prayer is often guilt-inducing. Not because we do not do it, but because we do not do it properly. We get bored; we rush it; we find excuses to reduce it; we give people short change; we let it drift; we are 'neither cold nor hot'. And all of this, to faithful Christian people who take their intercession seriously, is bound to result in that familiar Christian companion – guilt. Guilt, of course, is paralysing. First it causes us to hesitate awkwardly, and then we come to dread the confrontation with whatever it is that exposes our guilt. Surely there must be other ways to rekindle that fire of intercessory passion which is so essential to the effective mission of the Church. The last word cannot rest with guilt but with the God of new beginnings.

I have been outlining some of the problems associated with the task of intercession today. Whether the context of that prayer is the main act of Sunday morning worship, an all-age service, the small group, or the individual praying Christian, there are issues which are liturgical, theological, educational and emotional. What we lack are examples of good practice, and it is here that this book is hoping to make a small contribution.

First, however, let us just revisit some of the reasons why we believe this work of intercession is so central to the life and health of the Church, and, in the next chapter, look at some of the common conceptual problems about intercessory prayer, like:

- Why should we ask, if he already knows?
- How should we ask for things when we live in such a sceptical age?

5

- Who are we really asking, if it seems that this God has favourites?

Why should we intercede?

1 A deep instinct First, we intercede because it is one of the deepest instincts we have. Through time and civilization, through life and experience, the simple fact is – we ask for things. The Jewish novelist Isaac Singer once said in an interview: 'Whenever I'm in trouble, I pray. Since I'm always in trouble, I pray always.' When asked, 'Why are you in trouble?' he replied, in that classic Jewish style, 'Who is not in trouble?' Who indeed? And so it is a deep instinct to turn to the heavens and plead for generosity.

The obvious danger is that God is treated as a celestial cash-point, producing the required riches at the press of a few prayer-buttons. If the question about prayer is reduced to 'Does it produce the goods?' then we have abandoned the sphere of faith for that of the superstore. Nevertheless there is a touching and profound spiritual authenticity in the child who puts his head round the door and says to his parents 'I'm just off to say my prayers. Does anybody want anything?' We need to respect and work with this intuitive reaching out to a heavenly Father who wouldn't dream of giving his son a stone when he asked for bread (Matthew 7.9).

At the heart of this instinct to ask is the instinct to love. If we truly love people or care for them, we will want far more for them than we can possibly give. We will want their well-being in every respect, and so the very best we can do for them is to go before God on their behalf. Intercession is therefore a way of loving people. Seen in that way, when we say, on hearing of someone's difficulties, that we will pray for them, that is not a convenient religious sticking plaster that enables us to make good our escape; it is saying to that person 'I care for you enough to take on the serious task of holding you daily before God.' And then we had better do it!

2 A biblical invitation The second reason why we regard intercession as a vital part of being a Christian, is that it is the consistent expectation of the Bible that we will bring our needs and the needs of others to God. The direct conversations between God and his people recorded in the Bible are sometimes rather unnerving in their immediacy. To read about Moses' or Elijah's prayer life is like listening in on a telephone party line or the Internet. The discussion goes backwards and forwards, and God usually wins!

Nor does Jesus let us off the hook in the New Testament. His teaching about prayer emphasizes above all the immediacy of the relationship we have with God. He should be approached as *Abba*, Dad, the one I trust most deeply. We should ask straight out for daily bread, the essential sustenance we need, without feeling embarrassed at this show of self-interest. We should ask persistently, like a man waking a friend at midnight asking for some food for a visitor. We should ask, knowing that we will receive; seek, knowing that we will find; knock, knowing that the door will be opened (Luke 11.1–13).

The example of Jesus in prayer is similarly forthright. When he was faced with a human need he would often simply turn to his Father and ask (Mark 7.31–5, the healing of the deaf and dumb man; Mark 5.30–44, the feeding of the five thousand). Here is a vigorous, trusting and obedient prayer, and the implicit challenge of Jesus seems to be: 'Do you dare to pray like that?' Fortunately, one of the most exciting discoveries we make in intercession is that the Holy Spirit will be guiding and sorting out our prayers anyway: 'We do not know what we ought to pray, but the Spirit himself intercedes for us . . .' (Romans 8.26). This can give us a new confidence as we pray; the Spirit will interpret and mould our confused prayers so that they correspond with the loving purposes of God.

There is a godly confidence which we rightly claim when we go to pray for others. Not the arrogance of one who sets himself up as Chief Adviser to the Most High, but the confidence of one who knows he does not go alone into the courts of heaven, but enters with the covering authority of the Son and the interpretative wisdom of the Spirit.

In the hymn before the sermon a verger solemnly conducted the visiting preacher to the pulpit steps. He was just about to mount them when the verger held him back. 'Sir,' he said, 'we wait here for the Holy Spirit.' What is true of preaching is true of praying. We wait for the Holy Spirit. But having waited, we enter the halls of heaven with confidence, called by Jesus to pray with holy expectation.

3 A long tradition Intercession has always been at the centre of our public liturgies. Here is another good reason for continuing to honour that same centrality in our own day and our own practice. The Church has always seen it as a holy duty to bear the world to God in regular prayer. When the Church gathers, it intercedes. The core elements of the daily services (or Offices) said and sung by Christian communities through fifteen and more centuries have always been the reading of Scripture, praise to God, and prayer for the needs of the Church and the world. The service of Holy Communion responds to the reading of Scripture with the sermon, the Creed and then intercession: through the readings and their exposition we begin to see how serious is the world's need of God, and so we are driven to prayer.

It is important, however, not to take such prayer for granted or to be too flippant about its significance. Queen Alexandra, the consort of King Edward VII, was meeting a bishop at Sandringham railway station so that he could preach in the royal chapel. The motor car was still a great novelty and the Queen wanted to drive. She told the chauffeur to get in the back, and then turned to the bishop. Remembering the state prayers at Matins in all Church of England churches, she said: 'Don't worry, my Lord: twenty million people are praying for me now!' God has promised to take and use our prayers, but he asks of us not only faithfulness to the task of praying, but also a modicum of common sense!

It is clear, therefore, that we have both problems and necessities in this area of intercession. The problems are various, and have been outlined. The mandate is also very clear. What we must not do is allow our intercessory practice to drift into a spiritual malaise. The stakes are too high.

2 SOME FAMILIAR PROBLEMS

A woman was carrying a heavy tray of valuable china when she slipped and dropped it all on the floor. She sat amongst the broken cups and saucers full of self pity and found herself praying: 'O God, may that not just have happened!' A natural reaction, perhaps, but what does it say about prayer? Can it work backwards? If God is fully outside time then perhaps it makes a sort of sense, but thinking in this way may create all sorts of other theological problems.

About half way through the last chapter I posed a few of the classic problems about prayer. What some of the world's greatest minds and holiest spirits have wrestled with through many centuries is not going to be answered in a few pages written one damp March day in Durham! Nevertheless, unless we can have reasonable confidence that these problems do not have to end in a post-modern nightmare where no set of statements need have any relation to another set of statements, then we cannot pray with much real integrity. We may not be looking for definitive answers this side of eternity, but we can legitimately look for a positive provisional framework in which to hold our questions – and our praying.

Why should we ask, if God already knows the problems?

If God is God it is reasonable to assume that his information technology will be pretty impressive. At the very least he will know what is going on. So why do we have to go through all the bother of finding time, naming the problem, agonizing over what to pray for, waiting anxiously for the outcome, re-doubling our prayer, calling an all-night vigil and so on? We know that God's very nature is love; he wants nothing less than the very best for us. Is that not enough?

The point of our praying for situations of need is not that we are informing God of anything, still less that we are persuading him to do something he would not have done or had not thought of. The point of our praying is that it enables him to do what might otherwise have been more difficult. Such is his self-limiting humility in this world order that he works by collaboration rather than by edict. He respects the integrity of the way the world is, but his purposes can be taken further when his will and ours are tuned to a mutual resonance. The extraordinary truth seems to be that God depends on our co-operation for his kingdom to come, and when there is not that mutual resonance of wills, then neither God's best purposes nor our fallible desires can be realized.

Many is the time that as a father I longed to give my daughters information I thought they needed to know. (Who took the greatest number of wickets in a single test match? What was Blackpool's winning score in the 1953 Cup Final?) But there was no possibility of their receiving this important information until they themselves wanted it, until their wills and mine were in tune. Prayer is our way of laying hold of God's willingness, not overcoming his reluctance.

How should we ask for things when we live in such a sceptical age?

A Duke of Cambridge in the eighteenth century had the habit of responding out loud to prayers said in church. A clergyman was once praying for rain. 'No good,' said the Duke, 'not when the wind's in the east.' And that's the problem. What sense does it make to pray for changes in the way things are in a world like ours? Rain does not fall when the wind is in the east. A cancer is a cancer, and to pretend that prayer will reverse the course of the illness is only (it is said) to set ourselves up for a big fall. In any

11

case, we need the world to work in regular, consistent ways or else we would be at the whim of arbitrary change, not knowing when we could rely on the norms of gravity or thermodynamics. This is how the argument goes.

Let's put down a few markers. Certainly we cannot expect arbitrary interruptions of the natural course of events for our personal benefit. The dead of Auschwitz rule out the possibility of a cosy, domesticated view of how God relates to his world. But let's also recognize that there are no 'laws' of nature as such, just generalizations of observable experience. The fabric of creation has a much more open texture than we once thought. Nor, if we really get down to it, can a purely scientific account of an event claim to be fully comprehensive in its description. A physicist could describe your actions in reading this book very well, but not your purpose in doing so, or your awareness of what you are doing. In other words, the personal dimension of an event always eludes the observer; it cannot be captured on a computer print-out.

When we pray for things to change in a situation, therefore, we are not throwing pebbles at some iron wall of 'natural law'. We are co-operating with God in enabling his loving presence to come to bear on that situation, and so inevitably to affect it. When something unusual happens because of this, it is what one would expect. His presence does not negate or suspend all the other causative factors in that situation but it brings the particular action of God into that network of causes – a network which itself, of course, is already his. When these unexpected developments become particularly unusual we may talk of 'miracle', but this is still not a violation of 'natural law'; rather it is itself the 'natural law' of a deeper order of reality, what happens when we break through to the deepest modes of nature's operations. The supernatural is an infinite projection of the natural, to the point where it is transformed.

All of this may sound rather complex. And we must beware of claiming too much and attributing all sorts of events to God's direct action. Too often people have claimed a healing miracle, only to see the person deteriorate again and then to realize that it had just been a temporary remission. Nevertheless the biblical witness and centuries of Christian experience are quite uncompromising: when God is present different things happen, inevitably. Prayer is our part in those mysterious interactions, and in the gracious economy of God it is a vital part.

What is God really like, if it seems that he has favourites?

The church has been praying urgently for two people who both have leukaemia. Both are young, one in his thirties, the other a child. Everyone is deeply committed to prayer and loving action and the benefits are obvious: they are both in the middle of a network of support and care. But there is a vital difference. One gets better, the other dies. How is the church to respond to this? Is it all in the mystery of God's will? Or is God arbitrary, in which case how can he be trusted, or loved? What sort of God is this?

This is all part of the bigger problem of so-called 'unanswered prayer'. No one who takes their faith seriously can have avoided struggling with this most anguished of issues. As C. S. Lewis wrote, 'Every tombstone is a monument to an unanswered prayer.'

A few things can be said immediately. In the first place we may not receive the answer we want because our motivation is suspect. Not every request for a new Porsche gets answered! Further, we may be asking for the wrong thing. Billy Graham's wife Ruth once said, 'God has not always answered my prayers. If he had I would have married the wrong man – several times.' Moreover, we may think our prayers have not had a response because we can only see response in our terms. We may have received a quite different answer. We need also to remember that the people we pray for also have their free will and they may resist the best intentions of our prayers: God does not overrule our freedom.

Having said all this, however, the key problem we started with still remains. One person lived; the other died. Why? The short answer

13

of course is that we do not know. And that is not unreasonable. After all, we are Macbeth, not Shakespeare, the creature, not the Creator, and it is not surprising that the characters in the play cannot understand the mind of the author except by 'best guesses'.

The longer answer might look like this. When a couple experience the massive privilege and responsibility of producing a child they find they have created another human being which has its own radical independence. They can care for the child, love, encourage, persuade, and eventually reason, discuss, even argue with the child, but they can never start again and make this into a different child. She has her own way of being herself, and the parents have to recognize that they have limited their absolute power in the very act of creating her. Now they have *this* child and not *that* child.

Similarly, in the act of creating this cosmos God has given every part of it the radical independence it needs in order to exist apart from himself. God limits his power over it in the interests of love. He longs for every part of his creation to achieve its fulfilment, to become what it can become. Now, within that framework nature has that open texture we considered earlier, the possibility of human–divine co-operation which results in the unexpected, even the so-called miraculous. Nevertheless there must be intrinsic limitations to this open texture. God has made *this* world rather than *that*. We must somewhere come up against the 'is–ness' of things. Even God could not make square circles or dry rain.

It follows that when that church prayed for the two people with leukaemia they could not know where the intrinsic limitations lay, where it was possible and where it was impossible for the loving presence of God to be part of a process of physical healing. What is certain is that God was working flat out for both people. He was answering the praying of the church in all sorts of ways, seen and unseen, emotional, spiritual and relational. But in the one case, where the patient died, physical healing would have needed a different sort of creation.

If it seems to us, therefore, that God has favourites, we need to examine our understanding of God. If he is 'Abba', the loving Father who Jesus showed him to be, then we can have no doubt about his fairness and trustworthiness. He is utterly on our side, whoever we are. And 'if God be for us, who can be against us?' (Romans 8.31). We can pray to him with confidence, knowing that he will use our prayer in ways which are good, just and kind. We may not know precisely what will happen, but if God is unequivocally with us, then in some significant respect the situation we pray for will be changed.

One final word: if someone we are praying for does not get better, we should beware of blaming ourselves. Christians easily get on to a guilt trip about so-called 'unanswered prayer' (which does not exist – all prayer is used by God in some way). God is not waiting until we 'crack the code' and pray the right words. He does not hold off until we have built up a particular 'weight' of prayer and then give in: 'All right, you win. I'll do it!' He is the Prodigal's father, racing towards us at top speed. If our prayer does not seem to have changed anything, it is more likely we are up against the intrinsic limitations of a physical world which has its own created independence. And we should look more deeply: something will certainly have changed, although we can never predict what that will be.

Images of intercession

There is an important practical corollary from this discussion of how God answers our prayers. It is to do with how we mentally frame our prayers according to our understanding of what God is doing with our requests. In other words, we all have, whether we realize it or not, one – or a number – of controlling images which we use as we pray, images of who God is and how he uses our prayers. Different controlling images will reflect our theology, upbringing, personality and lots more, but it is worth taking time to consider the options and to decide whether we are happy with the particular images we habitually use.

Let us imagine we are praying for Tim. He is suffering from depression and we may bring him to God (that is already one image) in a number of different ways, each of which has its strengths, and some of which have their weaknesses.

Handing Tim over to God. Here we are bringing Tim to God and then handing over responsibility for him. It is an active, deliberate step, placing Tim fairly and squarely in the best hands. We might ask: do we then walk away, our job done? If we hand him over again tomorrow, does that mean he fell out of God's hands in the meantime?

Holding Tim before God. This time we are keeping hold of Tim, accepting continuing responsibility for him (the weight of him?) but presenting him to be the recipient of God's action.

Being with God with Tim on my heart. This approach to intercession sees prayer as more about 'being' than 'doing'. We can 'be with God' in a number of ways – sorrowfully, thankfully, in wonder, etc., and each describes a dimension of prayer. To be with God with Tim on my heart allows for continuing prayer for him, focused in moments when he is consciously named.

Holding Tim in the warmth of God's love. This image emphasizes the sensory experience of warmth as a legitimate metaphor for God's response to Tim's need. It has a stronger emotional content than some other images but may not appeal to those who see a danger of the Church using God as a spiritual hot-water bottle.

Keeping Tim tied to God's presence. The idea here is that prayer is the act of joining up, or tying together, particular needs and the fullness of God, who can meet those needs. It has the strength of letting God get on with whatever he wants to do, since all we do is bring them together. It also encourages confidence that Tim cannot fall out of God's care. However, the image of 'tying' usually implies a form of restriction or imprisonment, which is precisely not the purpose of praying for him.

Putting ourselves alongside Tim in loving concern. In this approach we are by Tim's side, sharing the depression, in empathy and concern. It has a more adult feel to it, in that it treats Tim as a friend rather than as someone who has to be 'carried' somewhere (like a baby?). On the other hand it underplays the active presence of God, leaving him as the unseen context of this encounter.

Seeing Tim through God's eyes. Here I am taking an even bigger empathic leap. I am looking at Tim as I imagine God does – with infinite care and compassion. I am trying to find the mind of Christ and to align my will with his. This does indeed correspond with a key understanding of intercession as trying to attune our wills to the will of God, but we might wonder whether 'seeing' is only a prelude to God's more active response and therefore whether this image goes far enough.

Taking my thoughts about Tim for a walk with God. This may seem to be one of the more fanciful images for intercession but its strength is in its active and discursive elements. It may appeal to the more extrovert personality which finds it hard to sit and concentrate on intercession for long. Here there is something to do, and you do not have to walk in a straight line.

Putting my care around Tim, and God's care around us both. This is a more embracing approach, carrying Tim in my heart but letting God carry us both. God is the nurturing parent, perhaps the mother, and all shall be well.

Storming the gates of heaven on Tim's behalf. Here the image is quite different from the others for here the scene is that of a spiritual battle where there is royal duty to be done. There is a vibrant sense of action, commitment and courage about this approach, but the weakness lies in the question about what or who is being stormed. A reluctant God? A sleeping deity?

Perhaps we can now see that the words we use in intercession all carry with them particular understandings of what is going on in prayer and what assumptions we are making about the character of God. More important, however, is that we get on with the task of praying itself. Making our prayers vivid, arresting and imaginative for each other is one side of the task. The other side of it is to make these prayers useful, faithful and beautiful for God.

In this chapter it has only been possible to skim the surface of some enormous theological issues. To follow these up more fully there is a list of useful books in the resources section. However, it has been important at least to offer an embryonic framework for these difficult questions if we are to proceed with the weighty task of intercession, whether that be in church on Sunday, in a small committed prayer group, or in the unseen spiritual traffic which goes on daily between us and God in private prayer. Nevertheless, the point about intercession is not to understand it, but to do it.

3 INTERCESSION IN PUBLIC WORSHIP

PRACTICALITIES

1 Decide what is special about this service. All Sundays and all gatherings for prayer have their own character. There may be a governing theme from the Church's year or from local church life. It may be a solemn occasion or a less formal service. What does the layout of the church do to the intercessions? Think your way into the mood of the church as it will be on that occasion. This is the context for the intercessions on that day and at that time.

2 Know your congregation. Think about what is likely to be on people's minds and hearts on this occasion. What concerns will they have from their lives outside church? What are the cultures they come from, and what therefore forms their world of ideas and values? Moreover, you should consider what emotional range they will be comfortable with in the ideas and words which you might use. It is no use being more emotional, pious, or 'flowery' than people are easy with; they will simply be embarrassed and shut off their concentration.

3 Pray about the real world and not about a narrowly religious one. People want to know that faith and life connect, and that prayer is relevant to the 167 hours a week they do not spend in church. Good intercessions demonstrate these connections and help people to live out their faith with more confidence during the rest of the week, because they see that God is Lord of these other worlds as well as their church world.

4 Be particular. Give examples from life: refer to news reports; name specific people; paint pictures with words; use images; be in touch with the world as it is. And avoid generalizations, repetitions and lists – the curse of so many prayers in church. On the other hand, beware of being so particular all the time that you limit the application of the prayers and trap others in your own world of ideas and concerns.

5 Use vivid language. Our use of language should avoid being conventionally religious, but should be rich, colourful and able to move people. Memorable phrases, with an occasional touch of beauty and poetry if possible, are a joy to listen to, even as they get to the heart of an issue and how we might pray for it. But remember not to go over the top.

6 Have a clear structure. Order and familiarity help people relax into praying. 'Sudden prayers make God jump', and sudden changes in the prayer structure make the congregation jump and feel unsettled too. This applies also to congregational responses. People like to know what is expected of them; often they are unable to get into the prayers because they are trying hard to remember the correct response and then they stumble over it when it comes.

Short responses are best – 'Lord in your mercy: Hear our prayer', or 'Lord hear us: Lord graciously hear us'. If a new response is to be used it should always be spoken over at the start: 'When I say the words "Let us pray to the Lord", please respond "Lord have mercy". [Short pause.] "Let us pray to the Lord: Lord have mercy".' The response can also be printed out on a service sheet.

7 Address prayers to God, and biddings to the congregation. And don't confuse the two. 'We pray for the strength that God gives . . .' is not addressed to God and is therefore not prayer. 'O God we pray for the strength that you give . . .' is quite different. Biddings, on the other hand, are rightly addressed to the congregation as a lead in to prayer itself: 'We remember this morning the disaster that we saw on the television news yesterday. Our hearts and our prayers go out to all those involved . . . [pause] . . . Suffering God, we pray for the victims of . . .'.

8 Pray; don't read notes. Even if you *are* reading them. The difference is in the intention of the heart. Even though we are naturally concentrating hard on reading the prayers well, the mind and spirit need to be directed towards God. People can tell the difference.

9 Use silence, and be prepared to take risks. Our services are often a torrent of words and ideas, far more than we can cope with, and many people are longing for some space. The intercessions are one obvious time when there can be pools of silence for people to rest in God, to find him and be found by him. More specifically, silence gives people the opportunity really to pray rather than to listen to someone else praying. People may be nervous of silence – particularly the leader of the intercessions! The golden rule is: don't panic! Give longer than you feel you can; go through your pain barrier. What will be happening is that people are getting used to the idea that this is serious prayer time, not an accident, and they will start to take up the challenge to pray themselves in the space offered. It needs clear signalling, with specific guidance on what to do. 'We'll be quiet to pray,' can leave people flummoxed. 'In silence, pray for one person you live or work with who needs God's help today,' may call out real committed prayer.

10 Use variety. Boring, predictable prayer makes God seem boring and predictable. What image of God are we then sending out, when in fact the invitation of prayer is to come into the most vital experience that this life affords – a relationship with the living God? This book attempts to offer a wide variety of different ways into lively intercession. Try them!

11 Look for training and feedback. The Church expends much energy on training people to preach, make music, take all-age services etc., but very little on leading intercessions. Look for help, and if it isn't offered, ask for it. A Saturday morning or two evenings of training once a year is not much to ask of a church which takes its worship seriously. It is also very helpful indeed to build in your own feedback system by having people you respect and who will be honest with you give you their considered evaluation of how effective the intercessions were. This is possibly the single most valuable thing you can do, both for yourself and for the church, to improve the quality of the vital ministry of intercession in public worship.

USING THE PRAYERS OF OTHERS

Often we will want to draw on the wisdom and insights of other people when we lead prayers in church. The occasions when we are most likely to use other people's prayers are probably morning and evening worship when it is not a communion service. Many fine prayers are contained in anthologies, and there is no need to reinvent the wheel. However, it is important that the prayers serve the current situation rather than be a set of formal and rather unreal petitions which have the effect of keeping God at a distance. There are a number of questions which the person leading the prayers needs to ask.

1 What theme should I follow?

Should it be a single theme (e.g. harvest or education or mission) or a multiple one (Church, world, community, individuals)? Is the theme given already by the season of the Church's year or have I got a free choice? What themes are on people's minds at the moment, or on the mind of the church locally (e.g. a building project, a new pastoral visiting scheme)?

2 What structure should I use?

A useful structure is:

(i)   bidding – a brief introduction to the need, e.g. 'On Education Sunday we have the opportunity to pray particularly for our local schools . . . for the staff, children, and all that goes on there week by week';

(ii) pause – a short silence to allow people time to focus on the schools in their own minds;

(iii) set prayer.

Usually four such biddings and prayers will be sufficient. Don't get carried away by having found so many lovely prayers you would like to use! The important question is: how can I best help the people of God to pray meaningfully on this occasion?

At the end, the Grace is often appropriate but should not be used as a kind of 'spiritual disinfectant' to keep the prayers in their place – at a harmless distance. Alternative ending prayers may be found in the Anglican Alternative Service Book (p. 105). Or try this:

> Lord, we thank you for hearing our prayers with the attentiveness of a loving parent. We ask you to take each need and answer each prayer in your own time and in your own way, for we know you to be just and true, and that we have asked in the name of Jesus Christ our Lord. **Amen.**

3 What sources of prayers should I consult?

There are many anthologies of prayers, ranging from the traditional to the avant-garde. There is a list in the resources appendix at the end of this book and it is worth choosing carefully and having a small selection on your shelves. Do not be tempted to buy each new glossy anthology. Each has a different character, and you need to find the few which will become really useful and familiar to you.

One of the most valuable things to do, however, is to start a file collection of those prayers that you come across which you find most helpful yourself. You will be able to use such prayers of quality with more conviction and imagination than the hundreds of other worthy prayers which leave you (and probably others) unmoved.

4 What prayers should I actually choose on this occasion?

Personal preference, instinct and spiritual discernment are the crucial factors when it comes to the selection of particular prayers. However, it is worth bearing the following in mind:

– prayers should not be too wordy and long, but crisp and to the point.

- prayers with memorable phrases and images are more helpful to the listener.
- it is good to have an eye for beauty in the prose as well as relevance in the topic.
- some classic prayers e.g., those of St Richard of Chichester, St Ignatius Loyola, St Teresa of Avila, have a lasting quality and bear repeated use. Novelty is not always best and familiarity can encourage real engagement in prayer.

NOTES FOR THOSE WHO WANT IDEAS TO DEVELOP THEMSELVES

This book is full of practical ideas for intercession but usually the idea is worked out in detail. Some people, however, do not want as much help as that; they are constricted by a fully worked example and would prefer just a few ideas to start them off. This section, and the next, are for them.

MODEL 1 *As used in Alternative Service Book, Rite A Communion intercessions*

Church You could pray about issues where the Church was in the news this week, or long-term issues facing the Church, or for particular church leaders. You might also pray for your local church and the needs and opportunities it faces in, e.g., evangelism, pastoral care, building projects.

World You could pray about the issues which are really in people's minds rather than the ones we feel we ought to trot out each week. What are they? What issues have left the front pages but still need our prayer? What are the issues coming up in the national or international agenda where we should be praying before the event rather than reacting afterwards?

Community We often pray well for both large-scale and small-scale events but not for those in the middle range, i.e., those which affect our local community. What is going on locally? What are the local needs of the homeless or young people? What are the local planning issues? When are the local elections?

The suffering It is good to be particular, but only after we have secured their permission to pray in public for them, or we are sure it has been given. Genuine space could be given for people to name those they know, in their hearts or out loud. Who, also, without being specific in naming people, are those who are easily missed out in prayer, e.g. long-term carers, gypsies, the hard of hearing, the victims of last year's accidents?

Those who have died Such people are remembered with thanks, or prayed for, according to the theology of the local church! Could some imagination be used – 'Elsie Tappin, who was here when the foundation stone of the church was laid and hardly missed a Sunday since . . .'? Long lists tend to be just that – lists, but the anniversary of people's deaths can be used well, particularly if genuine appreciation is given of what those lives meant.

MODEL 2 *Decreasing circles of prayer*

Creation and the environment You could pray for international initiatives on the environment, local action, current emergencies. It is important not to get too party political although some people will hear certain issues in that narrow context however careful you are. You could bring it home to practical personal responsibility by each of us as stewards of creation.

Nations in need Pray for particular countries, not just those the media are focusing on at present. Look for fresh angles, specific people who bear heavy responsibility. Avoid giving a news report.

Local community What are the issues locally? If you were not a Christian in church on a Sunday, what would be your concerns for the area in which you live? Pray for the schools, the local councillors, community groups, users of the church hall. Be specific.

Individual needs You could give thanks for good things in the church family this week as well as praying for needs. You could invite people to pray for events coming up – a church meeting, a birth, a youth event, an operation, the computerization of the church office. Again, beware giving notices to the congregation rather than praying to God.

MODEL 3 *The five marks of mission*
(Anglican Consultative Council 1990)

To proclaim the good news of the Kingdom You could pray for any form of outreach which the Church is involved in, locally or nationally, for those who have to answer for their faith in the media, for friendships with people who do not share our Christian faith – and perhaps give space for quiet prayer for specific friends.

To teach, baptize and nurture new believers You could pray for your church's policy on baptism and teaching, for people who are finding their way into faith, for the messages given by the church to newcomers, for a culture of encouragement in the church.

To respond to human need by loving service Pray for Christian Aid, Tear Fund, and other agencies; Christians in positions to influence political action for the poor. Pray for local initiatives in serving the community in whatever form they do - or do not yet – exist. Pray that Christians may be recognizable by the depth and quality of their caring.

To seek to transform unjust structures in society Pray for the prophetic role of church leaders in particular current debates. Pray for campaigning organizations pursuing justice, whether or not they claim the description 'Christian'. Pray that we may all be prepared to act symbolically for justice in our own lives and decisions, even on the smallest scale.

To strive to safeguard the integrity of creation You could pray for greater awareness of environmental issues and a more convincing stance from the churches. Pray for repentance and hope. Pray for a Christian critique of over-consumption, and genuine internationalism in political debate. Pray 'thy Kingdom come on earth' and ask for vision to sustain the struggle for the future of the earth.

MODEL 4 *Different aspects of a theme*

Many Sundays do in fact have a theme running through the worship, because it is a recognizable part of the Church's year or because it is implicit in one or more of the readings. This theme can be picked up and explored in prayer, taking a number of dimensions of the theme in turn. Several examples can be seen in the later pages of this section of intercessions. For example:

Baptism (p. 69):	people being baptized throughout the world; children born in the world's troublespots; people whose lives are not beginning but ending.
Advent (p. 52):	Christ coming in the Church; Christ coming in the world; Christ coming in the community; Christ coming to those in need.
Images of Christ (p. 92):	Christ the Light, the Love, the Peace, the Way, the Vine, the Resurrection.
Ascension (p. 64):	The message of Ascension in our faith, our world, our nation, our hearts.

NOTES AND PROMPTS

This section goes somewhat further than the last. Here you will find a number of examples of a standard outline of intercessions with notes to act as starters, and prompts for you to make the prayers appropriate for the particular day and context. In the first three of these examples you could 'mix and match' from one to another.

NOTES AND PROMPTS (1)

Let us pray for the Church and for the world, and let us thank God for his goodness.

Almighty God, our heavenly Father, you promised through your Son Jesus Christ to hear us when we pray in faith.

We pray for the life of the Church, especially

- *national church leaders, for wisdom and prayerfulness*
- *major issues and debates facing the Church, for honesty and fairness*
- *unity, love and fellowship in the Church*
- *local ecumenical relations and initiatives.*

Strengthen [. . . our bishop and] all your Church in the service of Christ; that those who confess your name may be united in your truth, live together in your love, and reveal your glory in the world.

Lord, in your mercy **hear our prayer**.

We pray for the needs of the world, especially

- *a troublespot in the news, for peace and a new start*
- *a country in longer-term need, for good government and international help*
- *the role of the United Nations, the Red Cross and other agencies*
- *courage and patience for those negotiating peace.*

Bless and guide Elizabeth our Queen; give wisdom to all in authority; and direct this and every nation in the ways of justice and of peace; that we may honour one another, and seek the common good.

Lord, in your mercy **hear our prayer**.

We pray for the well-being of our community, especially

- *local schools, their children and teachers, for vision and adequate resources*
- *local industries and employers, for stability and growth*
- *leisure and recreation groups in the area, that they may give good service and meet community needs*
- *the relationship of the church with all the above, for Christians to be actively involved.*

Give grace to us, our families and friends, and to all our neighbours; that we may serve Christ in one another, and love as he loves us.

Lord, in your mercy **hear our prayer**.

We pray for people who are in special need, remembering

- *those who are ill in the church family, for healing and comfort*
- *people with long-term learning difficulties, for patience and progress*
- *people who are lonely, depressed or suicidal, for good listeners*
- *people in our prisons and remand centres, for humane treatment and hope.*

Comfort and heal all those who suffer in body, mind or spirit; give them courage and hope in their troubles; and bring them the joy of your salvation.

Lord, in your mercy **hear our prayer**.

We remember those who have died, especially

- *church members or parishioners*
- *people whose anniversaries fall around now*
- *those who have almost no one to remember them.*

Hear us as we remember those who have died in the faith of Christ; according to your promises, grant us with them a share in your eternal kingdom.

Lord, in your mercy **hear our prayer.**

Rejoicing in the fellowship of all your saints, we commend ourselves and all Christian people to your unfailing love.

Merciful Father,
accept these prayers for the sake of your Son, our Saviour Jesus Christ. Amen.

NOTES AND PROMPTS (2)

The same framework as in the previous example can be used in this and the subsequent two sets of intercessions. Alternatively, the formal structure can be simplified with just the congregational response between each section. What follows here is another set of possible notes and prompts with the choice of framework being left to the leader.

We pray for the life of the Church, especially

- *our own church, for events and opportunities coming up*
- *local church leaders and councils, for wisdom and discernment*
- *church organizations, youth and children's work, for imagination, leadership, and growth*
- *the witness of the church in the community, for sensitivity and courage.*

We pray for the needs of the world, especially

- *Christians living out their discipleship at work, for Christ-centredness and the ability to relate their faith to workplace decisions*
- *Christians involved in politics, for Christian confidence and maturity*
- *the media, for ethical issues to matter to journalists and programme-makers*
- *the influence of films, videos and television on young people, for positive messages and images.*

We pray for the well-being of our community, especially

- *people who are feeling left behind and forgotten, the long-term unemployed, the old and the isolated, for everyone to be valued as unique*
- *social work and psychiatric agencies providing care in the community*
- *voluntary organizations of all sorts working tirelessly throughout the community, for a continuing flow of volunteers and energy*
- *every member of the community, for motivation to respond to need wherever it presents itself.*

We pray for people who are in special need, remembering

- *these in hospital and those awaiting treatment, for patience and prayerfulness*
- *people with major decisions to take, for wisdom and clarity of thought*
- *people known to us with private battles and challenges to face.*

We remember those who have died and those who are bereaved, especially

- *the victims of sudden death, and those they leave behind*
- *those who have suffered the death of a child*
- *those who listen to and counsel the bereaved.*

NOTES AND PROMPTS (3)

Here is another set of ideas to be used interchangeably with those above.

We pray for the Church throughout the world, especially

- *Church leaders in places of conflict, for wise interventions and generosity in their dealings with all parties*
- *growing churches in Africa and the Pacific rim, for the training of leaders and for spiritual maturity*
- *for any particular mission partner with whom the local church has a link.*

We pray for the needs of the world, especially

- *the delicate balance of the environment, for global awareness of the problems*
- *over-consumption of raw materials, for solid international agreements*
- *waste in our own homes, for care in the details of living*
- *respect for the beauty and design of nature as created and entrusted by God.*

We pray for our family and friends, especially

- *our closest family who have to put up with all our different moods*
- *the friends who have stayed by us through the years*
- *the friends we only keep in contact with through Christmas cards*
- *the quality of our own friendship to others.*

We pray for people who are in special need, remembering

- *those who are blind or partially sighted, for full enjoyment of God's world*
- *those whose deafness cuts them off from conversation, for understanding from others*
- *those with a progressive illness, for courage, the appreciation of each moment, and the knowledge of God's embrace*
- *those particularly on our own heart.*

We remember those who have died, especially

- *members of our own family, who gave us love and encouragement*
- *particular friends, who were taken from us too young*
- *any who died alone this week.*

NOTES AND PROMPTS (4)

This example takes the particular focus of baptism which often takes place in a main service when the church is gathered together. Again, material can be used interchangeably with ideas from the previous examples.

We give great thanks today for the baptism to new life in Christ of . . .

- *give thanks for the love and delight of the parents*
- *give thanks for the parents' godly initiative in bringing . . . for baptism*
- *pray for their homes as places of security and care, where . . . will learn a framework of lasting values*
- *pray for the families, that they may grow to appreciate ever more deeply the truth of the Christian story and the importance of the Christian community.*

We pray for the Church family here in . . .

- *pray that the church may be ready to receive . . . into its life*
- *pray for the church playgroup, crèche, childrens' work*
- *pray for the other young families in the church, for delight in parenthood and for Christ to be at the centre of their life together*
- *pray for those involved in baptism preparation, for sensitivity and clarity.*

We pray for new-born children everywhere:

- *for basic hygiene and nutrition where mortality rates are high*
- *for more international aid to be targeted to the poorest peoples*

>   *– for safety for children caught up in conflict, and settled homes for*
>   *those born in refugee camps.*

We pray for support for the family in our society:
>   *– for public policies and media treatment which encourage stable,*
>   *committed relationships*
>   *– for good theology to support the sacrificial loving needed in*
>   *family life*
>   *– for recognition of the number of different forms in which the*
>   *family comes today, and an understanding of the complexity of*
>   *the debate on the family*
>   *– for acceptance in the Church of people who approach tentatively,*
>   *looking for God, but with unconventional lifestyles.*

Lord we thank you again for the gift of . . . to enrich the human
family. Grant to their own families love and laughter, fun and
forgiveness, honest effort and lasting peace. And draw them, with all
your children, closer to your heart of love, for Jesus' sake. **Amen.**

INTERCESSIONS BASED ON THE SERMON

*Intercessions that come directly out of the sermon can be particularly
effective. This approach gives added meaning to both sermon and prayers,
and offers coherence to this part of the service. There is clearly no problem
in this if the preacher and intercessor are the same person; what follows
assumes that they are not. A counsel of perfection would be that the
preacher and intercessor get together at some point in the week to discuss
how the prayers can grow out of the proposed sermon.*

Key phrase

It may be that the leader of the intercessions can find out what the
preacher is going to use as the key verse or phrase. It has to be one
that has been well used in the sermon so that it is already

implanted in the congregation's mind, and will be instantly recognized as picking up the theme of the sermon. It can then act as a repeated anchor in the intercessions.

For example 'No one could say it was expected' (for a sermon on the Resurrection)

'No one could say it was expected.' But Easter is the festival of the unexpected . . .
'No one could say it was expected.' Lord, teach us to expect more from you . . .
'No one could say it was expected.' Lord, give people an expectation of peace in . . .
'No one could say it was expected.' Lord, give us expectancy as we meet in worship each week . . .

Headings

Sometimes there is a clear structure to the sermon which can be picked up in the intercessions. A meeting or a phone call to the preacher is all that is required.

For example
(1) A sermon on the need for forgiveness (i) in the family, (ii) in national enmities, and (iii) in our own relationship with God.
(2) A sermon on mission which starts in the church, goes out to the community, and then flows on to the whole creation.

Opening intercession

It is becoming fairly common practice among those well used to leading intercessions to pick up the theme of the sermon in the opening section of the prayers. This should not be attempted unless the leader has enough confidence, is clear what the sermon was really about, and can resist the temptation to put their own interpretation on the theme and in effect continue the sermon.

For example The sermon has been about the ascension and the lordship of Christ.

Dear God, we give thanks for the lordship of Christ, established now and forever above human affairs, above the Church, and above the Christian conscience. [*The three points of the sermon*] Give us grace to accept the lordship of Christ not just as an idea but as a living reality, starting here and now, with us . . .

EXAMPLES OF INTERCESSIONS FOR PUBLIC WORSHIP

The main body of this section is the practical worked examples of different ways of leading intercessions in public worship. None of these examples should be used! They are there to be adapted to the reader's particular situation and personal style. They are not set in stone, nor is the page corrupted by being marked with necessary changes (preferably in pencil). The hope is that readers will use these ideas as jumping-off points for their own creativity.

These ideas have necessarily arisen from the particular configuration of my own personality, background and tradition. Anyone else approaching this material, therefore, will be coming from somewhere else and should expect to want to change the intercessions which have come from me. We might remember, of course, that this is precisely the gap in which each of us is operating as we lead intercessions; our fellow pray-ers are equally unique in what helps them to pray, and our own preferred style will not quite be theirs.

(i) Standard intercessions

(1) STANDARD INTERCESSIONS

Later in this section of intercessions for public worship there are many examples of different ways of using this time of prayer. At the start, however, we will imagine settings which call for more straightforward intercessions where the worship is dignified and reasonably formal. Names, places and other details can be added as much or as little as wanted.

Let us pray for the Church and for the world, and let us thank God for his goodness.

Almighty God, our heavenly Father, you promised through your Son Jesus Christ to hear us when we pray in faith.

We pray for the witness of the Church this week, particularly in places where the Christian faith is ignored and forgotten. We pray for those who carry major responsibilities as bishops and church leaders, and are always expected to know what to say and do, whatever the situation. Give them compassion, wisdom and the mind of Christ.

Pause .

Strengthen [. . . our bishop] and all your Church in the service of Christ; that those who confess your name may be united in your truth, live together in your love, and reveal your glory in the world.

Lord, in your mercy **hear our prayer**.

We pray for Christians working in places of power and influence who make decisions which may affect many people. We pray for Christians in politics, the media, advertising and the financial markets, that they may know how to act and what to say, in order to be true to Christ. We pray too that we may examine our own power over others, at home or work, and use it responsibly, by offering it to the One who laid aside his power and took the form of a servant.

Pause

Bless and guide Elizabeth our Queen; give wisdom to all in authority; and direct this and every nation in the ways of justice and of peace; that we may honour one another, and seek the common good.

Lord, in your mercy **hear our prayer**.

We pray for those whom we love, the special people you have given to us, wherever they may be. We pray for our friends, the close ones and those we sometimes forget, those with a special problem and those who need you. We thank you for each of them and what they give to us. Keep us faithful to them as you are faithful to us.

Pause

Give grace to us, our families and friends, and to all our neighbours; that we may serve Christ in one another, and love as he loves us.

Lord, in your mercy **hear our prayer**.

We pray for those for whom this day will seem long and hard, for those in hospital or ill at home, those struggling with despair or depression, those waiting for a job, or important news, or a friend to call. We pray particularly for those for whom this day will be their last. We name in our hearts any people we know in special need.

Pause

Comfort and heal all those who suffer in body, mind, or spirit; give them courage and hope in their troubles; and bring them the joy of your salvation.

Lord, in your mercy **hear our prayer**.

We remember with deep gratitude those who have left their mark on our lives by giving us love and laughter, but have now gone before us to be with Christ. We hold them in our hearts, knowing that you, Lord, hold them in yours.

Pause

Hear us as we remember those who have died in the faith of

Christ; according to your promises, grant us with them a share in your eternal kingdom.

Lord, in your mercy **hear our prayer**.
Rejoicing in the fellowship of all your saints, we commend ourselves and all Christian people to your unfailing love.

Merciful Father,
accept these prayers for the sake of your Son, our Saviour Jesus Christ. Amen.

(2) STANDARD INTERCESSIONS

These intercessions use the same format as the previous one, but without the set prayers ending each section. Obviously the set prayers can be inserted, or any variation of them, together with appropriate details.

Let us pray for the Church and for the world, and let us thank God for his goodness.

Almighty God, our heavenly Father, you promised through your Son Jesus Christ to hear us when we pray in faith.

We pray for your Church today, gathering all around the world in tiny churches and great cathedrals, to praise you, to hear your holy word, and to meet you in bread and wine. Give us a sense of expectation as we come, and inspiration as we go. Help us to put our differences behind us and to unite instead behind the great commission of Jesus, to make disciples of all nations.

Pause

Lord, in your mercy **hear our prayer**.

We pray for a world which struggles to live justly and in peace. We pray for those who have to search for daily food or walk long distances for clean water. We remember with sadness those whose lives are cut short by disease or violence, and those who have fled their homes in fear. We pray for those who meet persecution and torture with courage and dignity. May your kingdom come and your will be done on earth as it is in the heavenly places.

Pause

Lord, in your mercy **hear our prayer.**

We thank you for those people who sustain us by their love and forgiveness. Thank you for the network of people with whom our lives are inextricably linked and who make up the fabric of our family and community life. Make us alert to each others' needs and quick to serve and encourage one another. May our gentleness with each other reflect your gentleness with us.

Pause

Lord, in your mercy **hear our prayer.**

We pray for those who are laid low by suffering and those who are experiencing the outrageous assault of pain. We trust your love for us and for all people, and your deep desire for our well-being. As we name in our hearts those who are in the grip of suffering, help us so to pray and to act that they may know your comfort and healing, both now and in the coming days.

Pause

Lord, in your mercy **hear our prayer.**

We thank you for those people who have given us the examples and models by which we try to live. We thank you for those who have lived and died in quiet holiness and whose prayers have helped to sustain the world. Help us to live in the light by which they lived, and to worship the source of that light, Jesus Christ our risen Lord.

45

Pause

Lord, in your mercy **hear our prayer.**

Rejoicing in the fellowship of all your saints, we commend
ourselves and all people to your unfailing love.
Merciful Father,
**accept these prayers for the sake of your Son, our Saviour
Jesus Christ. Amen.**

(3) STANDARD INTERCESSIONS

*These intercessions use the same basic shape as before but omit the formal
beginning and end and have a different congregational response. They can,
of course, be used with any other structure. Names of the sick or other
topical and local details can be added wherever wanted.*

The response to the words 'Lord, hear us' is 'Lord, graciously hear
us'.
Lord, hear us. **Lord, graciously hear us.**

Lord, we pray today for your Church, carrying a gospel of
forgiveness and freedom which is so much needed in our world.
Thank you for those with a gift for sharing this good news in
evangelism; thank you for those with a gift for sharing this good
news in the way they live. Give us the courage and the willingness
to be your witnesses in ways that are generous and respectful, and
which come from the overflow of our love and delight in you. Fill
us with your love, so that the world may believe.

Pause

Lord, hear us. **Lord, graciously hear us.**

We pray today for countries where there is war, random violence
or only fragile peace. Give to those who are trying to make peace,
an inner certainty of their calling and constant patience in their
negotiations. May hearts which have been darkened by violence

discover a different light and a better way. May the ways of diplomacy and the ways of forgiveness coincide at the conference table.

Pause

Lord, hear us. **Lord, graciously hear us.**

Lord, we pray for the spiritual health and welfare of our communities. First for the well-being of this our church community, that we may be a spiritual family, a household of faith, where people are welcomed and nourished. But we pray also for the social community of which we are part, that you would make it a place where all can flourish and the weak be cared for, where there is harmony and celebration, and a true civic pride. We pray particularly for those who lead this community by election, by position or by popular acclaim. May their leadership be that of the servant and their goals those of the Kingdom.

Pause

Lord, hear us. **Lord, graciously hear us.**

We pray for those who are going through times of trouble, some perhaps in our families, some in our church, some in our wider circle of friends. We know you to be both Lord and healer of your broken world, and we ask you to touch with your generous love all those who are on our hearts today because of their special need. May your love flood their lives with hope and healing, in spirit, mind and body.

Pause

Lord, hear us. **Lord, graciously hear us.**

Finally, Lord, into your hands we commit those who have run the race and kept the faith – even if that faith was known only to you – and now have gone to their reward. May your light shine upon them forever and our lives be richer because of their memory.

Pause

Lord, hear us. **Lord, graciously hear us.**

Keep us, Lord, in the joy, the simplicity and the compassionate love of the gospel. Bless us this day and those who you have committed to our care. Through Jesus Christ our Lord.

(4) STANDARD INTERCESSIONS

The set form of intercessions in the Anglican Alternative Service Book provides a coherent and comprehensive approach to prayer, even if the content is expressed in very different forms, as in the following example.

Brothers and sisters in God's family, let us pray for the Church and for the world, and let us thank God for his goodness and his many gifts.

God our Father, we remember before you the kaleidoscope of people we call 'the Church':

the busy Archbishop of whom everyone expects everything, but who most of all needs time to reflect and pray;

those who help organize our church and have so much to think about on Sunday mornings that they scarcely have time for their own worship;

the loyal [Sunday School teachers] who need ideas, patience, a sense of humour – and occasional thanks;

the older person who slips quietly in and out of church, and just needs to be there, uninterrupted;

the people sitting and kneeling near us now, known and precious to you.

May your blessing rest on each one.

Lord, hear us. **Lord, graciously hear us.**

God our Father, we remember before you the world's great needs and its unnoticed sorrows:

the countries where some are intoxicated with war, but most are desperately weary of it [particularly . . .];
the countries where a silent slaughter is still happening while the world's gaze has moved on [particularly . . .];
the countries of central Africa where great swathes of the population have been wiped out by AIDS;
the countries in deep need where children die for want of clean water and a spoonful of sugar.

May your blessing rest on each nation and all its people.

Lord, hear us. **Lord, graciously hear us.**

God our Father, we remember before you our families, friends and the communities where we live:

the person who has a special problem to deal with . . .
the friend who we have neglected for too long . . .
the neighbour who always looks so burdened and anxious . . .
[*local situation – e.g., the charity for the homeless that might have its funding withdrawn*].

May your blessing rest on each person and place, to renew and transform them.

Lord, hear us. **Lord, graciously hear us.**

God our Father, we remember before you individuals in need of hope, and we name them silently in your presence:

on our heart is someone in hospital or ill at home . . .
on our heart is someone suffering from depression or confusion . . .
on our heart is someone suffering from the multiple problems of old age . . .

but on our heart is also the memory of a Lord who loved and healed and saved.

May your blessing rest on each person we have named.

Lord, hear us. **Lord, graciously hear us.**

God our Father, we remember before you those who have died:

the close relation who we still miss;
the friend whose early death will always sadden us;
the people in the news who died tragically this week;
the child in a distant land, unknown to us but known and loved by you.

Grant us, with all who have known you in their hearts, a share in your eternal kingdom.

Merciful Father,
accept these prayers for the sake of you Son, our Saviour Jesus Christ. Amen.

(5) STANDARD INTERCESSIONS

These intercessions have a different shape from the previous four examples, although they cover the same ground. The congregational response is again different, but not difficult to pick up. Detailed concerns can be inserted wherever appropriate.

The response to the words 'Jesus, Lord of life' is 'in your mercy, hear us'.
Jesus, Lord of life **in your mercy, hear us.**

Lord, we give you thanks today for so many things, a thousand miracles we take for granted every day. Thank you for the vitality and diversity of the natural world. Thank you for the regularity and stability of the created world. Thank you for the way the body goes on functioning with such remarkable ingenuity. Train our hearts to be thankful so that we live daily out of a deep sense of gratitude and humility.

Jesus, Lord of life **in your mercy, hear us**.

We know that our world is both wonderful and flawed at every point. We see the symptoms of a disordered world in every news broadcast. Bless we pray those parts of the world which are especially damaged and in need of healing at the moment [remembering . . .]. Give them leaders of genuine calibre, and the support of the international community. And keep us from the sin of thinking that their problems are nothing to do with us, for we are all children of one heavenly Father.

Jesus, Lord of life **in your mercy, hear us**.

In the Church we hope to find a different way of living and sharing together, and so often we are disappointed. The flaw in creation is also in us and in the Church. Forgive us for distorting your gospel into our own possession and the likeness of our own prejudices. Give us joyful and generous hearts which allow you to work through us to bring meaning and beauty into your Church and world. Persuade as out of our arguments, inspire us out of our pettiness, and set us free to be agents of your Kingdom.

Jesus, Lord of life **in your mercy, hear us**.

We pray for people in any kind of need for whom this talk of 'life in all its fullness' would ring very hollow. Be close today to the lonely, the bereaved, the despairing and the desperate. Bless with hope those who are unemployed, homeless, deserted or friendless. Give your deep healing to the sick, the disturbed, the damaged and the lost. In our hearts we name in silence some of those who we know to be in dark places today . . .

Jesus, Lord of life **in your mercy, hear us**.

You, Lord, came to give us life, and to do so you had to lay down your own life to bring us back to God. Help us this day to live as those who have been given the glorious liberty of the children of God, and who want to live our lives in gratitude and joy. So make us ready for that day when all that is good is caught up in the life of heaven and Christ is all in all.

Jesus, Lord of life **in your mercy, hear us**.

(ii) Seasonal material

(6) ADVENT COMING

One of the great seasons of the Church's year is easily lost in the headlong rush to Christmas. Intercessions may help to hold up the process and emphasize the profound value of waiting and longing. A familiar structure for the intercessions may still be used, but each section can be imbued with the themes of advent.

Lord, prepare us for your Advent coming. In our prayers today we try to come to you, sure that you will come the rest of the way.

Lord, prepare us for your coming – in the Church.
Clean out the unnecessary clutter of our church life, the piles of dead habits, the cupboards full of prejudice, the cobwebs of compromise and the sad rota of forgotten dreams. Open our church to the free flow of your refreshing Spirit. Give to this church a new vision and hope. We want to belong to you again. [In particular, Lord, we long for this . . . *a special local plan or project.*]

Lord, in your mercy **hear our prayer**.

Lord, prepare us for your coming – in the world.
Come, drive away despair from our politics; revive our dreams of justice; restore our passion for what is good, right and true. Establish your just and gentle rule [in places like . . .] where peace has been powerless and violent people have had their day. Set a flame to the fuse of justice [in places like . . .] where arrogant people have defied the moral order year after year. Guard well the new springtime of hope [in . . .] where peace has come like a gift, wrapped in reconciliation and gladness.
[In particular, Lord, we long for this . . . *a particular world need.*]

Lord, in your mercy **hear our prayer.**

Lord, prepare us for your coming – in our own community.
In the problems of our locality help us never to forget the supremacy of love. May love motivate our care for this neighbourhood. May love heal the social ills which drag us into despair. May love inspire our citizenship to rise beyond mediocrity. We name in our minds the problems locally of which we are aware [particularly . . . *local issue*] and pray that love, gracious and practical, will find a way.

Lord, in your mercy **hear our prayer.**

Lord, prepare us for your coming – in those in need.
Give us eyes to search the face of the stranger and there to see the face of the Saviour. Give us sensitivity to hear the doubt and hesitation, and there, with that person, to share the confusion and the futility. There are those we know who are ill now, struggling this morning to handle the pain. Let us pray for them, for you come to us in them, and you ask for our love. We give that now, as we name them and love them in our hearts. What we have promised, in love and prayer, let us never forget to do.

Lord, in your mercy **hear our prayer.**

Advent Lord, come ever nearer. Come to rejuvenate our faith. Come to fortify our social conscience. Come to open wide our eyes of wonder. So that when the Saviour comes, he may steal into our hearts – and find them ready. Even so come, Lord Jesus. **Amen.**

(7) CHRISTMAS IS COMING

One of the keys to making prayer real is to use our imagination to put oneself in the mind and feelings of others and then to pray out of that empathic engagement. The following intercession is my own example, built around the varied ambiguous responses people have to Christmas. The repeated response of the words of the angel may be spoken by a second voice.

Christmas is coming. Keep watch with the housewives.
Already, she's afraid of Christmas. Afraid the money won't last; afraid the children will be disappointed; afraid of family rows; afraid of being tired; afraid of it all being too much.
Pray for her . . . *silence.*

Hear the words of the angel: 'Don't be afraid. I bring you good news, that will be for *all* people.'

Christmas is coming. Keep watch with the young people.
Already he's in overdrive. Planning parties – and partners. Buying luxury presents for those who don't need them. Filling time. Christmas exposes his emptiness. He has to keep running – in case the message gets through to him, and he sees himself as he really is – lonely and scared and very small.
Pray for him . . . *silence.*

Hear the words of the angel: 'Don't be afraid. I bring you good news that will be for *all* people.'

Christmas is coming. Keep watch with the old people.

Already she's fearful. It's such a lonely time. And it goes on so long. Christmas Eve, and excited families gather at home, but who will she be with that night? TV and a cup of cocoa. Christmas Day, and they'll fetch her for lunch, but is she really wanted out of love or duty? Christmas night: memories and regrets and feeling useless and alone.
Pray for her . . . *silence.*

Hear the words of the angel: 'Don't be afraid. I bring you good news that will be for *all* people.'

Christmas is coming. Keep watch with the clergy.
Already *he's* anxious. All these expectations. Carol services that are supposed to recapture people's innocence and nostalgia. Sermons that are supposed to send a thrill down people's spines. Bonhomie that's supposed to make *him* a cross between a TV host, Father Christmas and the Pope. And then that other anxiety – will the church be emptier this year – more excuses to think of, to cover the sense of failure.
Pray for *him* . . . *silence.*

Hear the words of the angel: 'Don't be afraid. I bring you good news that will be for *all* people.'

Lord, may Christmas be good news for millions of your anxious and tired people this year. May the angels sing for them. May Christ be born in them. May *your* love come home to them.
Amen.

(8) CHRISTMAS DAY

Christmas is a hard time to 'get it right' in public prayer; so many people have so many different emotions, ranging from elation to despair. One way of dealing with this is to opt for more spacious images, rather than be too particular and focused.

Holy Child, you come as the Sun to a world lit by candles.
We try so hard to make Christmas work well in our jaded
society. As we try to light our own way through the darkness
with matches and candles, so this Christmas may your great light
overtake us, and catch us up into your radiance. This wonderful
night/morning, deny us our familiar land of shadows, and grant us
the glory of the Sun.

Lord, in your mercy **hear our prayer**.

Holy Child, you come as the true Gift to a world full of presents.
The shops are empty; the Christmas stockings are full. The
Christmas trees could hardly shelter any more presents. And yet
only one Gift is necessary, as you steal into our lives and offer
your love. Help us Lord, both in the Church and in the world,
to recognize that mysterious Gift which you place in the crib at
our feet. Give us grace to receive that Gift, and be changed by it.

Lord, in your mercy **hear our prayer**.

Holy Child, you come with peace to a world in pieces.
We see, with you, the sorrow of the world, torn to pieces by
greed, fear and prejudice, those same things that took you from a
cradle to a cross. Come with the peace that always flows from
your wholeness to our brokenness. Fill our world with the joyful
hope that there is always a better way. This Christmas may the
peace of the young Prince of Peace embrace the world.

Lord, in your mercy **hear our prayer**.

Holy Child, you come with lasting joy to a world full of passing
entertainment.
As we settle down to watch long hours of television, give us still
the sense that there is a greater joy and a larger dream beyond
the flickering images. Let all creation hold its breath at the
arrival of a love beyond our calculation. When the Christmas

films have gone, may your joy remain, rooted and growing in our hearts.

Lord, in your mercy **hear our prayer**.

This *night of nights/day of days* we celebrate your coming, holy Child of Bethlehem. Open our ears to the angels' song and our hearts to their message. May our generosity reflect yours and our delight know no bounds. For in our joy we share the joy of heaven, now come down to earth.

Glory to God in the highest, and on earth peace, goodwill to those on whom his favour rests. **Amen.**

(9) LENT

These intercessions depend on the imaginative use of one controlling theme, that of spring-cleaning. The hope here is that in addition to the benefit of praying in church, worshippers may take away with them an idea which will inform their own continuing thought and prayer afterwards.

The response to the words 'Lord of Lent' is 'renew our lives'.
Lord of Lent **renew our lives**.

Lord of Lent, come to your Church and ask us your hard questions. Are we faithfully proclaiming your gospel? Are we demonstrating in our life together the justice of your Kingdom? Have we welcomed the weak and given prominence to the poor? Come to your Church to spring-clean our ways of life, our structures and our priorities. Point out to us the cobwebs, the dirt, the extravagance and the waste. Create in us a clean heart, O God, and renew a right spirit within us.

Lord of Lent **renew our lives**.

Lord of Lent, come to the nations and challenge our idolatries. Spring-clean the sordid cupboard of this world's false gods. Sweep out the false pride, the self-seeking, the deceit, the corruption and lies. May the kingdoms of this earth seek justice, peace and the integrity of creation. May we look beyond immediate advantage to seek the common good, and be drawn to it, as a lark to the dawn. [Especially we ask for your cleansing hand in . . .]

Lord of Lent **renew our lives**.

Lord of Lent, look with compassion on those whose minds are full of anxiety and bewilderment. We remember people who are lonely, imprisoned, despairing and humiliated. Clear away from them all unnecessary feelings of fear, guilt and self-hatred. Assure them that when you spring-clean our hearts and minds you know what you are doing, for you have been there, one of us, and you are to be trusted.

Lord of Lent **renew our lives**.

Lord of Lent, turn your healing love towards those who are sick and in pain today. We have in our hearts some known to us, some known to the Church, and some known only through the news. We bring them to mind now . . . Clear away from them, we pray, those things that hurt, harm and hinder them. May your healing touch still have its ancient power.

Lord of Lent **renew our lives**.

For ourselves, Lord, we pray that your spring-clean would be thorough and true this Lent. Show us clearly those effortless sins we no longer even notice, and help us to address the sins which sit on our shoulder every day, our constant companions. Give us both discipline in dealing with some faults and gentleness in dealing with others, and help us to know the difference. Create in us a clean heart, O God, and renew a right spirit within us.

Lord of Lent **renew our lives**.

Renew our Church, renew our world, renew our hearts,
our cleansing Lord of Lent. **Amen.**

(10) GOOD FRIDAY

*This is a day when prayer can be very effective, or very banal. The
crucifixion is not so much a puzzle to understand: it is more a mystery to
enter into. It may be, therefore, that the best way of praying on this day is
through images and meditation rather than through intercession. The
following way of doing it is particularly dependent on being read slowly
and carefully.*

Lord Christ,
On the cross, on the nails, you loved beyond reason and forgave
    beyond measure.
On the cross, on the nails, you gave the forces of evil their notice
    to quit.
On the cross, on the nails, you soaked up this world's sadness like a
    sponge in vinegar.
On the cross, on the nails, you lost – and won – in a single,
    glorious throw of the dice.
On the cross, on the nails.

In the hands, in the side, you felt the misery of this world's cruelty.
In the hands, in the side, you endured the hammer blows of the
    world, the flesh and the devil.
In the hands, in the side, you experienced the pain of tortured,
    disfigured humanity.
In the hands, in the side, you lost the power to live, and won the
    right to glory.
In the hands, in the side.

Through the sweat, through the blood, we see the eternal face of a
    suffering God.

Through the sweat, through the blood, we glimpse the anguish of
the crucified Creator.
Through the sweat, through the blood, we begin to believe the
impossible is happening.
Through the sweat, through the blood, we begin to know that our
God saves to the uttermost – and then beyond.
Through the sweat, through the blood.

In the darkness, in the darkness
all our prayers have died,
save this:
Lord Jesus Christ, Son of God, have mercy on me, a sinner.

*An extended silence follows, or music, e.g. Vaughan Williams, 'The Lark
Ascending' or Taizé, 'All you who pass this way' (from the cassette
Pentecost).*

(11) EASTER

*A helpful approach to praying at the great festivals of the Church is to use
one of the evocative images of the biblical story as the theme which runs
through the intercessions. In the following example the powerful image of
the stone which was rolled away from the tomb is paralleled with the need
for stones to be rolled away from some of the tombs in which we live.*

In these intercessions, to the words 'Lord, come in love' please
respond 'and roll away the stone'.

Lord, come in love **and roll away the stone**.

Many people did not know why last Friday was called Good. To
them it was just another holiday and a few shops inconveniently
shut. Many people knew it was a religious festival, but which one?
Many people knew it was the day Jesus died, but they couldn't
say why. Many people, one Saviour of them all. The stone of
un-knowing lies heavy across the tomb.

Lord, come in love **and roll away the stone.**

Lord, so often it seems that we have locked up your truth in the Church so that only we can understand it and share its bright colours. We guard our packages of belief and our ways of doing things and we hope you understand that it is in your best interests. Truth is too valuable to risk in the open market; it might get mixed up with prostitutes and sinners. The stone of un-belief lies heavy across the tomb.

Lord, come in love **and roll away the stone.**

In our hearts, Lord, there is sometimes resentment, even this glorious Easter time. We resent our ill-fortune, the success of others, the joy we nearly had. On a bad day we resent the lottery being won by someone else and the fact that our football team always loses. We know it to be wrong, but resentment is an old friend; it is hard to shake him off. This old stone of resentment lies heavy across the tomb.

Lord, come in love **and roll away the stone.**

We each know good and lovely people this morning who are up against it; and even some people who are not so good and harder to love. It will help our prayers if we name them specifically in our hearts now . . . The stone across the tomb is an illness, or grief, or breakdown, or a major decision. You, Lord, know the weight of these stones that lie heavy across the tomb.

So Lord, come in love **and roll away the stone.**

Mighty God, high King of Easter, bringer of joy and hope, take from us our doubt and disbelief this Easter; make us witnesses of your resurrection as we see the stones roll away from the tombs we have named. This we ask in the name of your risen Son, the ever-living Jesus Christ. **Amen.**

(12) A SUNDAY AFTER EASTER

Often it is good to use a familiar phrase from a biblical narrative as a recurrent refrain. It gradually works its way into the heart. In the following example it works best if there are two voices leading the intercessions because then the challenge of the refrain is addressed to the congregation, rather than being used by them to unknown recipients. Fill in details in the spaces provided or elsewhere.

VOICE 1   It is some time now since Easter. Those were heady days. Our risen Lord was fresh from his grave, and all creation sang a new song. But now April moves on, a new term's work for some; several more months before the holidays; another late blast of winter; ordinary Sundays of ordinary worship; the dull hand of unexpectant prayer.

VOICE 2   Christians, think again. Why do you seek the living among the dead?

VOICE 1   Lord, we must be looking in the wrong places. Open our eyes to see you, alive and smiling, in the heart of our worship, in the word of the preacher, in the lift of the music, in the taste of the sacrament. Help us stand on tiptoe as we listen, sing and pray, knowing that at any moment we may be touched by your own hand and raised up from our dull vision.

VOICE 2   Christians, think again. Why do you seek the living among the dead?

VOICE 1   The world is weary, and so soon after its Lord was raised. There is heartache [in . . .], conflict [in . . .], hunger [all over . . .]. So soon we lose the Easter hope of a new creation, and a new people energized to love in the world's dark places. We look at our past failures to cope and we expect more of the same. Teach us hope and give us joy as we dare to think new thoughts and devise new plans for your suffering children.

VOICE 2   Christians, think again. Why do you seek the living among the dead?

VOICE 1   Forgive us, Lord, for our cynicism about politics and our politicians. We expect so little of them it is not surprising they live up to those expectations. Help us instead to seek the living among the living, living hope among living political systems. Make us prayerful and supportive of our politicians, especially now as they face hard decisions [about . . .].

VOICE 2   Christians, think again. Why do you seek the living among the dead?

VOICE 1   Lord, we often tell you how little you can do in a situation, asking you to bring a little comfort here and a little healing there. We seek your help in the dry world of our dead expectations. Instead we ask you today to be our living Lord in our living hope [for . . .]. We will keep silent before you now and pray for our special situations and special people, with expectancy in our prayers . . . *longer pause.*

VOICE 2   Lord, we promise to think again. We will pray in hope and expectation. We will seek your living presence not among the tombs, but in the bustling heart of life. And we know we will see you there, in Galilee, for you will be there before us. We will no more seek the living among the dead. For you are risen. Alleluia!

(13) ASCENSION

The following intercession takes the great theme of this Sunday and explores different dimensions of it, a useful approach to many Sundays of the year. It then uses familiar lines of a hymn to hold the prayers together in an easy rhythm. This different form of response would have to be carefully introduced at the start or be printed on the news sheet.

At the name of Jesus   **every knee shall bow.**
Every tongue confess him **King of glory now.**

Lord we need the message of Ascension in our church. Sometimes we get very small-minded: we are upset if things are not done the way we like. We are easily discouraged by failure or small numbers. And sometimes our vision is as low as newly cut grass. Give us confidence not in our church but in your Church, not in our faith but in your gospel, not in our success but in your Ascension.

At the name of Jesus   **every knee shall bow.**
Every tongue confess him **King of glory now.**

Lord, we need the message of Ascension in our world. As we struggle towards the millennium we are aware of more violence, hunger, pollution and despair than ever: of torture used as normal practice; of 1,500 children dying of hunger in the time that we are in church this morning; of an ever bigger hole in the ozone layer. But we pray that we may also hear other truths, for your gospel tells us of an ascended Lord and an invincible Kingdom; of a God who will with certainty reconcile all things to himself.

At the name of Jesus   **every knee shall bow.**
Every tongue confess him **King of glory now.**

Lord we need the message of Ascension in our nation. Our culture is tired, tired of political systems which promise but do not deliver, tired of instant fun that feels good but does not satisfy; tired of inventing new values that collapse at the first touch; tired of religion that promises bread but gives a stone. Put into our hearts an irresistible confidence that all is not as it seems, that love, truth and integrity are never defeated, that the kingdoms of this world will indeed become the Kingdom of our God and of his Christ. For,

At the name of Jesus   **every knee shall bow.**
Every tongue confess him **King of glory now.**

Lord we need the message of Ascension in our own hearts. Too easily our God is so small; we lift our eyes to the hills instead of the high mountains. Too easily we fail to expect you to be present in our worship, to speak in our hearts, or to change anything in response to our prayers. Too easily we remember our weakness, and forget your strange and beautiful strength. Take us back to the deep truth of a crucified, risen and ascended Lord, so that we may fall joyfully to our knees again and taste the wonder and certainty of his love.

At the name of Jesus   **every knee shall bow.**
Every tongue confess him **King of glory now.**

Amen, amen, our God reigns!

(14) IMAGES OF PENTECOST

Pentecost is a festival when we ought really to expect God's presence with his people, so it may be appropriate to attempt a genuine waiting on God, so that he can reveal himself as he wants and as we are able to discern him. People need to be prepared for this as follows.

After each section of these prayers there will be a substantial period of silence. Please use this time to wait on God and to pray for whatever the Holy Spirit brings to your mind. Do not rush into

prayer, but listen carefully for the prompting, the nudge, of the
Spirit . . .

Holy Spirit, come as fire, and burn away the sins that cling to our
church
    come as fire, and burn away the conflicts that divide and
        depress us
    come as fire, and burn away our pettiness, our insularity, our
        small gospel
    come as fire.

Silence

Holy Spirit, come as wind, and blow away the bureaucracy that
tries to put you into a box
    come as wind, and disturb our best-laid plans which left you
        out
    come as storm, and rage through our hypocrisy and cowardice
        till all is clean
    come as wind.

Silence

Holy Spirit, come as floodtide, and water the dry ground that we
call our spirituality
    come as floodtide, and sweep away our ramshackle defences
        against your love
    come as floodtide, and fill every nook and cranny of our lives
    come as floodtide.

Silence

Holy Spirit, come as life-giver, and put again to us that basic
choice – life or death, blessing or curse
    come as lifegiver, and build our confidence that the last word
        in a resurrection faith is always 'life'

come as lifegiver, and touch our jaded faith with the miracle
of Christ
come as lifegiver.

Silence

Spirit of the living God, fall afresh on us.
Spirit of the living God, fall afresh on us;
break us, melt us, mould us, fill us.
Spirit of the living God, fall afresh on us.

(15) TRINITY SUNDAY

*Sometimes the theme of the Sunday gives us the structure for our
intercessions and we do well to accept it and work with it. Trinity Sunday
gives us many prompts for our prayer; the Celtic beginning and end are
optional!*

Ever One, Sacred Three,
Holy God, the Trinity.

O God beyond us, lead us forward to pray.
O God beside us, teach us gently to pray.
O God within us, still our hearts to pray ... *pause.*

Holy God beyond us,
you create and sustain all things, but only by the power of self-
giving love.
We celebrate your creativity this morning, the risk and imagination
you demonstrated in making such wild diversity in the world: the
rhinoceros and the dragonfly, the Himalayas and the spider's web,
the earthworm and the human brain. There is mystery and joy at
the heart of creation. Holy God beyond us, we celebrate the
mystery and the joy which is found even in us ... *pause.*

Son of God beside us,
you never leave us comfortless.
Always you walk with us, neither too far ahead nor a step behind.
And you teach us the love songs of the Kingdom.
Bless, we pray, those who have not noticed that you are there
beside them, or who have chosen to ignore you.
Bless those who are dying of loneliness and those who need you so
desperately.
In the quiet, we name one or two such people before you, and
pray that they will raise their eyes to see you. Son of God beside
us . . . *pause.*

Holy Spirit within us,
always you are seeking to infiltrate our lives with peace and
strength;
always you are trying to give us more of yourself.
And yet we often feel empty and afraid, and so does the
community of nations.
Fill, we pray, all those dark, dank places of this world with your
warm life:
[. . .] where violence terrorizes the people;
[. . .] where hunger stalks the land.
And where there are people we know in whom hope is running
low, be for them a summer breeze and a spring of fresh water. Holy
Spirit within us . . . *pause.*

O God beyond us, give us faith.
O Christ beside us, give us peace.
O Spirit within us, give us life.

Ever One, Sacred Three,
Holy God, the Trinity.

(iii) Special events

(16) WHEN THERE'S A BAPTISM

These prayers may or may not take the place of the prayers in the baptism service. They fit in particularly when the baptism is part of a Communion service and the prayers are intended to have a wider reference than the baptism family alone.

Lord, we are delighted to welcome [*names of children*] into the Church today. People worldwide are flooding into your Church – tens of thousands every day. And you love each one of them as if there was only that one to love.

> Here is a child baptized in the heart of England, one of the most difficult places to be a Christian.
> Here is a child baptized in a village in Russia, where the Church is just finding its feet again and trying to give Russia back its soul.
> Here is an adult baptized in a river in Korea with a hundred others, and here is a teenager baptized in central Africa in a great celebration that lasts for hours.

Lord we pray for this multitude of people, of all ages, colours and sizes, who are pouring into your Kingdom today.

Lord, in your mercy **hear our prayer**.

Another child has just been born in Northern Ireland. She doesn't know whether she's Catholic or Protestant.
Lord, grant that it may never matter.
Another child has just been born in [*troublespot*]. He's too small to pick up a gun.
Lord, grant that he may never need to.
And yet more children have just been born in every country in Africa.
Lord, grant them simply a future.

Lord Jesus, you said 'Let the children come to me and don't ever try to stop them.' Thank you for the world's children – all of them.

Lord, in your mercy **hear our prayer**.

In the midst of life we are in death. Even as we welcome these new lives into the Church across the world, we are saying farewell to many others:

> the much loved grandfather with the crinkly smile and a hundred stories;
> the businessman who worked too hard and forgot how to stop;
> the little child whose body never really got going;
> the lady who came to the early service and really carried the whole church, because she prayed for everyone so much.

Lord, each of us can picture in our mind's eye one special person who we have had to relinquish into your extraordinary love. As we picture them, we love them . . . and you are good, and your love is endless, and you are to be trusted . . . Make our voices one with all the baptized, in heaven and on earth.

Lord, in your mercy **hear our prayer**.

As those who have been baptized into Christ, may we all enter into the liberty and splendour of the children of God, through Jesus Christ our Lord. **Amen.**

(17) MOTHERING SUNDAY

On Mothering Sunday the Church is faced with a difficult balance. On the one hand we do not want to be too sentimental and reinforce stereotypes; on the other, there is a genuine desire in most people to give thanks for their mothers, as is clear from the commercial success of 'Mothers' Day'. 'Mother Church' embraces us all, of course, but even here we must be careful not to reactivate older notions of dependency.

In our prayers today, when I say 'Lord in your mercy', please answer 'hear our prayer'.

Lord, in your mercy **hear our prayer**.

On this special day we ask your blessing on our closest relationships. We give thanks for the love and protection of parents for their children, and in particular for the way mothers care for and nurture their families. We ask for your strength and patience for parents who find bringing up children to be particularly stressful.

Lord, in your mercy **hear our prayer**.

On this special day we ask your blessing on our families. At home we are most truly ourselves, and seen at our best and our worst. Give us grace to be able both to forgive and to be forgiven, and to learn the value of honesty, fairness and gentleness in all our close communication.

Lord, in your mercy **hear our prayer**.

On this special day we ask your blessing on those for whom family life has meant anguish and disappointment. Please heal their painful memories with the loving presence of your Spirit, and give them grace to step hopefully into their future.

Lord, in your mercy **hear our prayer**.

On this special day we give you thanks for the Church, which has been there for us from our childhood up. Thank you for the good things in the Church which have nourished us and helped us to grow – the love, the extended family, the holy food of Communion. Make us mature members of the Church, able to give back our love, our time and energy, that the Church may continue to make real the good news of Jesus.

Lord, in your mercy **hear our prayer**.

On this special day we give you thanks for your tender strength as you offer to carry us all, in our human families and our church family, into the joyful maturity of the children of God. We praise you Lord, and ask you to bless us.

Lord, in your mercy **hear our prayer**.

(18) HARVEST

Harvest is one of those festivals when it is difficult to pray in ways that are fresh and avoid being trite. One answer is to start with what is immediately before people in church, or familiar at home, and then to broaden the range of the intercession until the needs of the world come into focus. Local colour will always help to make the intercessions more vivid.

The response to the words, 'For what we have received' is 'make us truly thankful'.

For what we have received **make us truly thankful**.

Abundant God, we saw and smelt your generosity even as we entered church today. Thank you for the riot of colour, the astonishing tastes, the wild shapes. You spared no expense in your creativity; you tried every trick and they all worked. Thank you for every brilliant idea which we see before us in the harvest today.

For what we have received **make us truly thankful**.

The harvest spills over into our homes. Our cupboards and fridges are full of good things from around the world, and our meal tables are never short of quantity or choice. Year by year this abundant earth pours forth its amazing harvest. And yet, generous God, so often we give you little thanks.

For what we have received **make us truly thankful**.

We remember this morning that people have worked hard, sweated, hurt their backs, and endured all weathers to get this food to us: honest toil and sometimes exploited labour. And then there were packers, shippers, refiners, warehousemen, lorry-drivers, shop assistants – all have passed on your good gifts to our tables. They deserve our thanks much more often than once a year. So . . .

For what we have received **make us truly thankful**.

Lord, when we next take a tomato from the fridge, or cut a slice of bread, or pour some rice into a pan, bring to our minds in humble gratitude the chain of production that got that food there; give us imagination to appreciate the complexity of our interdependence with the rest of the world, and finally let our minds pause in grateful contemplation of your abundant, profligate love.

For what we have received **make us truly thankful**.

As we enjoy your rich harvest here, we remember with sorrow and regret that our over-consumption in the West is at the expense of others. Your good earth produces enough food for everyone, but not for everyone's greed. Strengthen the hands of the aid agencies; reorder the priorities of governments; and move the hearts of us all to recognize the face of Christ in the plight of the hungry.

We keep a time of quiet now to think and pray as we are led; to give thanks for another wonderful harvest; to pray with longing for a fairer world. In silence let us pray to the Lord.

Long pause

Merciful Father,
accept these prayers for the sake of your Son, our Saviour Jesus Christ. Amen.

(iv) Creative ideas

(19) THE BREAKING OF BREAD AND THE POURING OF WINE

These intercessions make use of repeated images which are at the heart of our Sunday worship. The details of the prayers may be constantly rewritten, but the power of the central images of the breaking of bread and the pouring of wine should remain helpful and effective. The three-fold form of the response may be difficult to pick up and so it may be best to have those three lines printed out on the weekly news-sheet. It should also be rehearsed at the start of the intercessions. The key to the congregational response should be pointed out as being the phrase, 'we encounter your love'. If it looks too difficult to get right, the leader can of course say the whole refrain, or a second voice can join the leader.

Lord, we encounter your love
in the breaking of bread
and the pouring of wine.

Sometimes we are not sure why we come – habit, duty, the easiest option. Sometimes the hymns are empty, the words are dull, and we don't really concentrate. Quite often the mind wanders off to the Sunday papers or what has to be done this afternoon. Wouldn't it be nice to be a happy pagan? But then, Lord

we encounter your love
in the breaking of bread
and the pouring of wine.

Around us is a world of extraordinary wonder and terror. People are discovering love and losing it. Some are striding forward confidently and others are walking on broken glass. Some are full of hope, and some are crushed and exhausted. And always the burning, pressing beauty of God is coming to meet us.

Lord, we encounter your love
in the breaking of bread
and the pouring of wine.

Each of us brings our own special people to this service, carrying
them in our hearts:
the child we despair of, and the child we long for;
the parent we love [and perhaps resent], but who can no longer
live alone;
the friend whose cancer has wrecked her life.
We bring them with us, Lord, because

we encounter your love
in the breaking of bread
and the pouring of wine.

In our deepest places there are hidden fears, and thoughts we
admit to no one. All our vulnerability is exposed there; all the
darkness which waits in our dreams. Perhaps we can begin to see
that nothing is unknown to you, and that you look with mercy,
not with blame. We come ourselves, Lord

to encounter your love
in the breaking of bread
and the pouring of wine.

Gracious God, in this service we come to break bread for the
city and pour wine for the world. We break bread for our sin and
pour wine for our celebration. We break bread for each other
and pour wine for your Kingdom. Bless us and all those for whom
we pray

that we may encounter your love
in the breaking of bread
and the pouring of wine.

(20) CIRCLES OF PRAYER

These intercessions depend in part on people having a visual imagination. The idea of circles, however, is an easy image to hold and readily allows people to widen out the scope of their prayers stage by stage. The risk is worth taking!

Let us for a moment think of our prayers as being like circles in a pond, made by throwing a stone into the water. The surface of the pond is still and silent; the stone drops into the middle, and we see the first circle emerge.

In this circle are the people closest to us – family, friends, the irreplaceable ones. There aren't many in this first, small circle, but we know them well, their strengths and their struggles, their enjoyments and their special needs. Let us pray for them.

Silence

The circle spreads. Look now at the second circle. Here are the people we know well, perhaps work with, go out with sometimes. Here there may be more distant members of the family whom we don't make contact with as much as we ought, but we care for them none the less. Here are neighbours, friends from a while ago, people who send us Christmas cards. And there are many needs; let us remember some, and pray for them.

Silence

The circle spreads again. Look now at the third and fourth circles. People we know less well. We see them at the school gate, every day we exchange a friendly word. We meet them in the shop, or out with the dog, or we greet them in the pub. There are hundreds of people out here in these circles, too many to pray for individually. In any case, we don't know their needs. But they are known to God; he has loved them from their birth. Let them be washed by these circles of prayer.

Silence

The circles spread right out. They reach the edge of the pond; one after another they lap against the banks. Our prayers extend to the ends of the earth, for all God's creation is the object of his mercy. Our prayer is an act of love for the world. Let us delight to encompass all things within the circle of God's extraordinary care and keeping. In these far circles, hold everything in the love of the Father.

Silence

Lord God our Father, our prayer this morning is a small pebble thrown into a large expanse of need. We thank you that your love is greater still, and we entrust every circle of our prayers to your generous mercy and grace, through Jesus Christ our Lord.

(21) NEXT WEEK'S NEWS

If we are to pray about what is really on people's minds then we have to take the material of the daily newspaper and television news into our prayers. This is an attempt to do so but it depends on careful delivery and enough of a pause being left for people to bring their concerns out of their memory and into genuine prayer.

As ever, this week we have been bombarded with news – home and overseas, political and personal, tragic and trivial. Our minds easily close down, resisting the assault of so much news. But some images, stories and issues get through our defences and linger in the mind. We can take this as God's call to us to pray for these issues. Let us think what news stories are on our minds this morning. Pray for them now in the silence, asking God to be fully present there, in judgement, mercy or grace . . . *pause.*

Lord, in your mercy **hear our prayer**.

Last week there was other news; some earlier chapters of long running stories, some one-day wonders, some tragedies, easily forgotten by us, but just as sharp and painful for the sufferers now as then. Let us try to remember what stories were on our minds last week . . . The needs go on, and so should our prayers. Let us pray now that God's grace may continue to be at work there, healing and renewing . . . *pause*.

Lord, in your mercy **hear our prayer**.

This time next week the papers will be full of new stories, the TV giving us new images. New faces will be looking out at us; there will be new incidents for the pundits to debate. Let us pray now for one such area of concern or one section of society that is likely to crop up in next week's news – the Government, our church leaders, countries in difficulties, people in trouble. Pray for whatever God gives you to pray about as you look ahead to next week . . . *pause*.

Lord, in your mercy **hear our prayer**.

O God, set your blessing on us all as we begin this week together – on our world, our church, our community, our family and friends. Heal your suffering ones, raise up your broken ones, inspire your joyful ones. And give yourself afresh to us, as with all our sisters and brothers, we stand before you in hope. For Jesus' sake. **Amen.**

(22) MISSION AND EVANGELISM

People are often fearful of evangelism; the word triggers an overdose of English reticence! It may be possible to build prayer in this area more gently by starting with the personal experience of every Christian. As always, the leader must know his or her congregation, and what resistances there may be.

Father, we thank you this morning that we are here in church at all.
  Someone first helped us to understand what the Christian faith
    was all about
  Someone first helped us to know your love.
  Someone first took the risk of sharing their own faith by what
    they did or said.
We thank you for that person, or those people, through whom we
first made contact with a living faith. We thank you for them now,
in the silence of our hearts . . .

Lord, in your mercy **hear our prayer**.

Father, we know that the Church will die in this generation unless
people go on doing what was done for us – sharing their faith in
action or explanation.
  We pray for those who have a special gift for making the gospel
    relevant and attractive [particularly . . .].
  We pray for those who have a special way of living that draws
    others to Christ.
  We pray for those who have a special opportunity for mission
    coming up soon [particularly . . .].

Lord, in your mercy **hear our prayer**.

Father, we acknowledge our own diffidence in sharing our faith –
the fear of embarrassment, of seeming manipulative, of losing the
trust of friends. Give us instead, hearts full of love, and lives centred
on Jesus Christ, so that our words and actions are all of a piece and
always Christian. So may we find ourselves naturally talking of
Christian things, or talking of other things Christianly:
  in the way we respond to stories in the news;
  in the way we handle issues in the workplace;
  in the way we defend the weak;
  in the way we care for the wounded;
  even in the way we answer the question 'What did you do on
    Sunday?'

Lord, in your mercy **hear our prayer**.

Father we pray that this week we shall not be ashamed of being
Christians:
    that we shall not disown you or your standards;
    that we shall not ignore the honest question.
We pray that this week we shall be glad to know you as Lord:
    that we shall relax in the sheer normality of belonging to you;
    that we shall speak of you and act for you with courtesy and
        integrity.
Give us we pray the dignity that was in Christ Jesus as he spoke of
his Father's love.

Merciful Father,
**accept these prayers for the sake of your Son, our Saviour
Jesus Christ. Amen.**

(23) MISSION AND SOCIAL ACTION

*It is easy to make our prayers for society's problems either bland or
repetitious. Our intercessions need to be fresh and up to date, detailed but
not narrow, clear but not simplistic; and we should not blanch at the
possibility of being thought 'political' – the gospel is bound to have social
implications.*

Let us come to God today with a concern for mission and social
action, remembering that he is interested not simply in collecting
Christians, but in renewing creation.

Lord, give to your Church we pray a profound concern for the
well-being of the world you made. Guide our church leaders into
judgements that are just and compassionate. Give them words
which are wise and incisive. They have to speak for the Church at
the moment about so many different issues [such as . . .]. May they
have time to ponder, experts to give them good advice, and the
insight which comes from you alone.

Lord, in your mercy **hear our prayer.**

Lord, give to us also we pray, here in this church, a full and rounded gospel, so that we engage properly with our locality rather than seeming to shout at it. Give us a concern for the well-being of our schools and teachers, for the quality of our community life and local councillors, for the treatment of our weak and marginalized members. [And here we pray in particular for . . . *issue in the community*.]

Lord, in your mercy **hear our prayer.**

Lord, we know that it is so much easier to relate our faith to our interior life, and our home and church life. But your vision is so much bigger. What use is a cosy church if society around us is in despair? Open our minds and hearts to confront the darkness with justice, and to embrace the broken with love. Here in our imagination are many people:

- a black family who dare not leave the house at night: we pray for them . . .
- a gay Christian whose inner conflict nearly drives him to despair: we pray for him . . .
- a young woman whose childhood abuse has ruined her relationships with men: we pray for her . . .
- an old lady who only got two cards at Christmas, still on her mantelpiece in June: we pray for her . . .

Lord, we pray that you will give to the gospel we proclaim the radical edge that we see in the words and actions of Jesus, who came not to be served but to serve, and not to save his life but to give it up in the cause of the Kingdom.

Merciful Father,
accept these prayers for the sake of your Son, our Saviour Jesus Christ. Amen.

(24) GUIDED SILENCE

Many people long for more silence in worship since they feel bombarded with words and events. Others feel threatened by silence since they do not know what to do with it. Both groups can therefore be helped to enjoy and value silence if they are carefully led into intercession based on ample space to pray quietly. The great temptation in the leader will be to cut short the silence after the first rustles are heard! This pressure should be resisted. People need to know this space is genuine and that the prayer really is up to them. Of course, the leader should add whatever examples are appropriate to prompt prayer.

Our minds are so often full of words, and what is worse, our hearts are often clogged up with thoughts and ideas as well, which leaves little room for meeting God in simplicity and stillness. So this morning we are going to have space to pray ourselves, guided with leads and prompts.

So first, let us take a little time to notice how many good things surround us, how much there is that we take for granted, and how much our lives have been blessed this last week with good people and enjoyable experiences.

Silence

We pray now for some of those people and places in the news, things we will read in the Sunday papers when we get home, or maybe have seen on our TV screens during the week. We hold them now within God's love.

Silence

We turn now to pray for the Church, for any of the big issues facing it at present [such as . . .], and we pray for our own church, particularly with many opportunities and some problems before us [for example . . .]. We ask for guidance and grace for the Church.

Silence

Between us all, we know so many people who are struggling today with illness, crises, big decisions and major changes in life. God's care for them is even greater than ours, but let us show our own love and concern for them as we pray, naming our own people in quiet trust before God.

Silence

Each of us has things on our mind, perhaps things we hesitate to mention to anyone else. But our heavenly Father understands us totally, and wants only the very best outcome for us. Let us pray to him in the honesty of our own hearts.

Silence

These, Lord, are the prayers of your people this morning. We ask you to take each one of these prayers and answer them in your own time and in your own way. And in the meantime give us expectant and trustful hearts. For Jesus' sake. **Amen.**

(25) CIRCLE US

Celtic imagery is especially appealing to many people today. One effective image used well by David Adam in his books of Celtic prayers is that of being circled by the loving, protective presence of God. The following intercession needs to be read carefully, with adequate pauses between the sections, so that the repeated 'Circle us' is striking rather than irksome.

Circle us, Lord.
Circle our Church with the light of the gospel.
May we understand more of our faith and why we believe it.
May we understand more of our doubt and not be too hard
    on it.

May we commit ourselves to following you in the small details
of our lives; in this particular fellowship, and at this particular
time.
Circle us, Lord. Keep light within; keep darkness out . . .

Circle us, Lord.
Circle our nation with the values of the gospel.
Give to our national institutions – Government, the law, the
health service, the unions, the Church – give them the values
of justice, fair representation, concern for the weak, equal
opportunities for every person.
And may the sheer generosity of your presence infuse our
national life with hope and encouragement.
Circle us, Lord. Keep hope within; keep despair out . . .

Circle us, Lord.
Circle our family and friends with the love of the gospel.
Keep them in peace and security. Guard those of our loved
ones who are vulnerable; strengthen those who are struggling;
encourage those who are on the brink of something new.
We name these, our special people, in our hearts now . . .
May the deep peace of the Prince of Peace keep them all.
Circle them, Lord. Keep love within; keep danger out . . .

Circle us, Lord.
Circle the sick and the bereaved in your healing presence.
There are some we know who are simply not well; some who
are fearful and in pain; some who are on their last journey.
Circle them now Lord, the very people we name in our hearts
or aloud, circle them in the healing presence of Christ . . .
May the touch of Christ be for them the touch of wholeness
and healing.
Circle them, Lord. Keep peace within; keep fear out . . .

Circle us, Lord. Our hearts, our homes, our church, our nation,
our world.

Circle us, and let us never slip outside the enchantment of
your grace, for Jesus' sake. **Amen.**

(26) PRAYERS FOR A BRUISED PLANET

*Prayer gives us the chance to expand our vision and to glimpse God's
passion for his planet. This form of intercession tries to bridge the gap
between the individual in the pew and the Church's ultimate task of
renewing creation. It depends on the congregation using their imagination to
rise continually higher over the world; some will find this easier than others.
Again it is important not to rush the silences, for that is when the prayer is
made. The details are only suggestions and can be adapted to local
situations.*

In our prayers today we are going to try and link the detailed
needs of our own church with the great purposes of God for the
whole of creation.

Imagine if you will that you are standing outside this church of
ours, looking at its familiar shape, and thinking of all it represents –
the worship week by week, the daily prayer which no one sees, the
spiritual energy which inspires people for their weekday work, the
groups which meet here, the good works done. All the rough edges
of that wonderful motley band of Christians that make up this local
church of ours.

Now try and see this church as God sees it, and loves it. In silence,
pray for the life of this church, mentioning in particular any special
concern you have about our church life now ...

Now rise above the church and see the whole *parish/area/town/
village.* Look on the whole of it and be aware of its vibrancy; all the
myriad activities, people washing cars, people on the golf course,
people arguing, some crying. There are plans being made over
breakfast tables and shops opening their doors. There are people
sitting anxiously at bedsides and children totally absorbed in their

85

games. This is our place, with its streets and parks, its schools and offices, and also with its stories and myths, its history and its dreams.

Now try and look down on this *parish/area/town/village* and see it as God sees it, and cares for it, for everyone without exception. In silence, let us pray for this place, in whole or in part, holding it in the warmth of God's good will and purpose . . .

Now let us rise higher still, and see in the eye of our imagination, this whole country, with all its teeming vitality, its beautiful countryside and its struggling cities [from Pennine moorland to Trafalgar Square, from Salisbury Cathedral to Birmingham backstreet]. We see a nation rich in talent, low in confidence, loving its sport, addicted to its television, largely content to live without God. We know in this land that the poor are in difficulties, that our institutions are creaking, that it is hard to be a good politician, that materialism is our major faith.

Look down on this land of ours and try to see it as God sees it, not with favoured nation status, except that every nation is at the centre of his loving attention. See this land bathed in the love and grace of God . . .

And now let us rise very high, and see our whole world, as if seeing it from space. A small, colourful ball, blue and brown and smudged with cloud. The earth, our home. So insignificant, and yet so densely packed with life and purpose. A world of infinite richness and complexity, and needing very careful looking after. A world that has gone to the brink of global war, has interfered recklessly with its finely balanced natural systems, has made extraordinary progress and yet been immeasurably cruel. A world that has chosen to go its own way, ignoring the Maker's instructions.

Try and see this bruised planet as God sees it, precious in grand design and in minute detail. See it and pray for it. The Kingdom of God is a healed creation . . .

God so loved the world . . . that he gave his only Son.
Amen, Amen.

(27) A LITANY OF LIFE

Litanies are reassuring in their rhythm and repetition. The following litany builds a picture of prayer through the years, drawing on the loving presence and action of God at every stage. People need to be told that each sentence in the litany is short and so they need to be ready with the response 'Hear us good Lord'.

Sisters and brothers in Christ,
    let us come to the Lord in hope,
    let us pray to the Lord in faith,
    and let us hold to the Lord throughout our lives.

Lord, keep safe the new-born baby who struggles for life in the hospital incubator.

Hear us, good Lord.

Give reassurance to the child unnerved by the sound of his parents arguing.

Hear us, good Lord.

Guard well the teenager tempted to gain acceptance by taking drugs at a party.

Hear us, good Lord.

Guide clearly the young woman who is not quite sure if her current man is really the one to be her partner for life.

Hear us, good Lord.

Give patience to the young man who could make money so much more quickly by bending the rules.

Hear us, good Lord.

Be close to the young parents, both delighted and stretched to the limit by their first child.

Hear us, good Lord.

Give hope to the distraught mother, frightened by her anger with her crying baby.

Hear us, good Lord.

Call back the tempted husband, following his instincts towards another woman.

Hear us, good Lord.

Give self-confidence to the man in middle age, redundant, bewildered and afraid.

Hear us, good Lord.

Bless with reassurance the middle-aged woman who wonders if she took a wrong turn some time back.

Hear us, good Lord.

Open the heart of the embittered 50-something year-old who was passed over for the better job.

Hear us, good Lord.

Give freedom and hope to the woman who retired early but is not sure whether she should be elated or depressed.

Hear us, good Lord.

Guard closely the lonely, the sick and the dispirited, and touch them with your deeper wholeness.

Hear us, good Lord.

Keep watch with those coming close to their destiny, afraid of the pain and unsure of the future.

Hear us, good Lord.

And so in your mercy gather to yourself every faithful believer, and those whose faith is known to you alone, and present us all, complete in Christ, to the joy of your coming Kingdom.

Hear us, good Lord.

Yes, hear us, good Lord.

(v) Prayers from the life and work of Christ

(28) THE WORD BECAME FLESH

This incarnational theme can be used on many occasions, not just around Christmas. The need to 'embody' our Christian caring in practical action is a standing challenge to the quality of our discipleship. The method used here is that of mulling over one key verse: 'The Word became flesh and dwelt among us . . . full of grace and truth' (John 1.14).

VOICE 1 The Word became flesh and dwelt among us.

89

VOICE 2 Lord, may our love become flesh this week. May our
love have skin on it, as yours did in the person of Jesus.
May our love not falter:
when somebody's problem seems too great for us even
to start helping;
when we are tired and just do not want to listen to
those closest to us;
when we are fed up, and want other people to notice
our own needs for a change.
May our love become flesh.

Pause

VOICE 1 The Word became flesh and dwelt among us.

VOICE 2 Dwell among us, Lord, this week. May we never be able
to escape your dazzling presence.
Dwell among us as we work, where we usually don't
think of you, but need you all the same.
Dwell among us at home, when emotions run high
and we are angry or hurt.
Dwell among us in church, when we are tempted to
consult everyone, except you.
Dwell among us in our closest relationships, where
yours is the bond of peace and joy.
Dwell among us this week.

Pause

VOICE 1 The Word became flesh and dwelt among us, full of
grace.

VOICE 2 Lord, may our lives be full of grace this week:
full of grace, when we feel rejected, ignored or
forgotten;
full of grace, when we really want to be bitter and
jealous;

full of grace, when we dare to say what we actually
    feel;
full of grace, when you set before us the Prodigal we
    know we should forgive.
May our lives be full of grace this week.

Pause

VOICE 1 The Word became flesh and dwelt among us, full of
grace and truth.

VOICE 2 Lord, may our words be full of truth this week:
    truth which challenges hypocrisy and cowardice, even
        amongst our friends;
    truth which upholds the rights of the powerless, the
        poor and the neglected;
    truth which does not count the cost, but acts
        according to conscience;
    truth which speaks with humility and integrity, and
        without arrogance or malice.
May our words be full of truth this week.

Pause

VOICE 1 The Word became flesh, and dwelt among us, full of grace
and truth; and we have beheld his glory, glory as of the
only Son from the Father.

VOICE 2 Lord, may we behold your glory this week. May we see
the divine splendour behind the ordinary events of our
lives. And as we see the depth and meaning of things, so
may we live with more awareness of the sacred, and so
with more joy and reverence through all our days. May
the glory belong to Christ, in whose name we ask it.
Amen.

(29) CHRIST THE LIGHT, THE LOVE, THE PEACE, THE WAY

These intercessions demonstrate the value of a clear pattern (here based on images of Christ) and of repetition (here based on the ideas of pouring and showing). A framework which quickly becomes familiar can be a great aid to prayer. Not every section need be used, or others could be substituted. Again, specific places and people can be mentioned at any point in the prayers.

Lord, you are the Light that the darkness can never conquer.
　　Pour your light into the darkness of [*this world*], so that people can see better ways of solving problems.
　　Pour your light into the confusion of [*our national difficulties*], so that people can see new strategies and possibilities.
　　Pour your light into us, your quarrelsome children, for we ourselves are part of the darkness.

Lord, in your mercy **hear our prayer**.

Lord, you are the Love that casts out fear.
　　Pour your love into the hearts of all of us who lose our temper and are tempted to torment our children.
　　Pour your love into the hearts of all who have been abandoned or let down and who vow they will never love again.
　　Pour your love into the troubled minds of those suffering mental instability and who do not know which voice to obey.

Lord, in your mercy **hear our prayer**.

Lord, you are the Peace that the world cannot give.
　　Pour your peace into the United Nations and its Security Council, that peace may be the goal of their work, and peace the method of getting there.
　　Pour your peace into the soul of this community in which we live, so that people may believe the rumour that you are alive.

Pour your peace into our own hearts as we try to live out our heavenly citizenship in an alien land.

Lord, in your mercy **hear our prayer**.

Lord, you are the Way that leads to the Father.
Show us your way through the problems that face the nation at the moment, [*particularly* . . .].
Show your way to those who are seeking a life of meaning and integrity, but who have not yet looked to you.
Show your way to us here, that we in this church may know the next steps in our pilgrimage of faith together.

Lord, in your mercy **hear our prayer**.

Lord, you are the Vine, whose branches we are.
We pray for those we know who belong to this part of the vine but are at present having a difficult time, for whatever reason. We pray for them in silence or out loud . . .

Lord, in your mercy **hear our prayer**.

Lord, you are the Resurrection and the Life and we are your Easter people. Take these our prayers and answer them in your own good way in the power that flows from your risen presence. We ask this in the joy of our Easter faith. **Amen.**

(30) I WILL BE WITH YOU ALWAYS

Many biblical phrases can be used as the anchor for intercession. The following example is probably best used with two voices, rather than with a leader and a congregational response. The repetition and clear structure should ensure that people feel secure and able to pray through the words and ideas offered.

VOICE 1 Jesus says: I will be with you always, to the end of the age.

VOICE 2 Jesus: be with the Church, the holy Church, the sinful
Church, your Church;
> be with the suffering Church, especially in [. . .] where
> the odds are stacked against faithful Christians;
> be with the clergy here, bearing a hundred burdens
> that the rest of us do not see;
> be with the lay people here, trying to live out the
> gospel in the ambiguities of home and work;
> be with us in our church life here, especially as
> [. . . *local task or need*].

VOICE 1 Jesus says: I will be with you always, to the end of the age.

VOICE 2 Jesus: be with our nation, our confused nation, our
talented nation, our materialistic nation;
> be with those left behind in the pursuit of money,
> powerless before TV's flickering fantasies;
> be with the school-leavers looking out at an empty
> horizon;
> be with the homeless, who have found that an
> Englishman's home is his cardboard box;
> be with our nation, especially this week when
> [. . . *national event or need*].

VOICE 1 Jesus says: I will be with you always, to the end of the age.

VOICE 2 Jesus: be with the weak who know their need of you;
> be with the strong who do not know their need of
> you;
> be with the sick for whom life is anxious and painful;
> be with the lonely who are desperate for someone to
> call their name;
> be with these people who we name before you
> now . . .

VOICE 1 Jesus says: I will be with you always, to the end of the age.

VOICE 2 Jesus: be with the joyful whose hearts are overflowing with gratitude;

be with the newly engaged for whom life is a great promise;

be with the newly promoted, who have had their talent recognized;

be with the newly converted, who have found a faith for life.

VOICE 1 Jesus promises to all who will listen: 'I will be with you always, to the end of the age.' Lord, help us to believe your promise, and to live in that confidence. **Amen.**

(31) LITANY OF JESUS

This litany focuses on the many names given to Jesus in the Bible, and allows prayer to engage with those dimensions of human experience which are echo-ed in the life of Christ. The leader can choose how much of the litany to use, and what to change, to make it appropriate to the congregation.

Jesus, Word of the Father, speak for those who have no voice and stand by, powerless, while others play with their lives.

Lord, hear us. **Lord, graciously hear us.**

Jesus, child of Bethlehem, remember now those children who are born to struggle, whose mothers have no milk and whose fathers have no bread.

Lord, hear us. **Lord, graciously hear us.**

Jesus, refugee in Egypt, remember those who have been terrorized out of their homes, and now try to sing their own song in a foreign land.

Lord, hear us. **Lord, graciously hear us.**

Jesus, carpenter of Nazareth, remember now those who work with their hands but see their jobs being taken over by computers and technology.

Lord, hear us. **Lord, graciously hear us**.

Jesus, teacher of Galilee, remember now those children who think they cannot learn, that success is always for someone else, that theirs is a lost cause.

Lord, hear us. **Lord, graciously hear us**.

Jesus, friend of the poor, be a friend to the invisible poor in our neighbourhood, those we never notice, the empty and lonely ones, the exhausted and silent ones.

Lord, hear us. **Lord, graciously hear us**.

Jesus, healer of the sick, remember now our broken humanity, and touch with your tender love all those who cannot trust their bodies to be whole.

Lord, hear us. **Lord, graciously hear us**.

Jesus, light of the world, remember now those whose sight is growing dim, and who fear the dying of the light.

Lord, hear us. **Lord, graciously hear us**.

Jesus, door of the sheepfold, remember now those other sheep of yours who feel the Church is not for them because they are not good enough, or cannot understand the language, or do not know the entry code.

Lord, hear us. **Lord, graciously hear us**.

Jesus, bread of life, take us, pray over us, break us open and share us out, that the Church may feed and fill the world with your generosity.

Lord, hear us. **Lord, graciously hear us.**

Jesus, prophet of Jerusalem, speak judgement to our complacency, cry aloud to our disobedience, that the manipulator, the torturer, the abuser, the destroyer, may turn back to your ways of justice and peace.

Lord, hear us. **Lord, graciously hear us.**

Jesus, man of prayer in Gethsemane, remember now those who are overwhelmed by the prospect before them, and are on their knees with nowhere else to go.

Lord, hear us. **Lord, graciously hear us.**

Jesus, victim on the cross, remember well those who hang there beside you, martyrs and fools, heroes and villains, victims of murderous regimes and people who were in the wrong place at the wrong time.

Lord, hear us. **Lord, graciously hear us.**

Jesus, risen in the garden, bring us to the terror and beauty of your risen presence, that we may be an Easter people of unshakeable hope.

Lord, hear us. **Lord, graciously hear us.**

Jesus Christ, ascended Lord, work through, and watch over, our bewildered society, that the kingdoms of this world may become the Kingdom of our God and of his Christ.

Lord, hear us. **Lord, graciously hear us.**

Jesus Christ, Lord of all, sun of righteousness, rock of ages, lamb of God, living water, true vine, dayspring, messiah, Lord and King – come again, come again in glory.

Even so come, Lord Jesus.

(vi) Using music

(32) MUSIC IN INTERCESSION

There are a number of ways in which music can enhance the effectiveness of intercession in public worship. Some are relatively straightforward; others require more talented musicians or more time to prepare.

1 Musical responses can be used to break up the prayers into sections. The response should be sung through, led first by the choir or music group and then sung by everyone. Then follows the first section of the intercessions, coming clearly to an end so that the musicians are able to come in confidently, even if the congregation are a bit timid. So the intercessions continue. Taizé chants can be especially helpful, but with imagination many other short choruses and chants emerge as possibilities.

(i) O Lord hear my prayer, O Lord hear my prayer;
When I call, answer me.
O Lord hear my prayer, O Lord hear my prayer;
Come and listen to me.
(from the tape *Laudate!* Taizé, 1984)

(ii) Ask and it shall be given unto you,
Seek and ye shall find,
Knock and the door shall be opened unto you,
Allelu, Alleluia.
(from 'Seek ye first' in *Mission Praise*,
Marshall Pickering, 1990)

(iii) Through our lives and by our prayers
your Kingdom come.
(from *Come All You People*, Wild Goose
Publications, 1994)

(iv) Listen Lord, listen Lord, not to our words but
to our prayer.

You alone, you alone understand and care.
(from *Come All You People*, Wild Goose
Publications, 1994)

(v)   Remember, remember your mercy Lord
Remember, remember your mercy Lord
Hear your people's cry as they call to you
Remember, remember your mercy Lord.
(from *Let's Praise*, Marshall Pickering, 1988)

2 **Variations** on this theme include:
 – an individual soloist singing the response, or singing the first
   phrase with everyone else joining in the second phrase:
   Soloist: Through our lives and by our prayers
   All: Your Kingdom come.
 – the chant (especially suitable for Taizé refrains) played quietly
   but continuously on instruments (or on tape) behind the
   said prayers, and rising at the end of each section for the
   sung response to be taken up. The said prayers may need to
   be spoken through a microphone.

3 **Opening and closing music** can be helpful, the music at the
beginning drawing people closer to God, and the music at the end
summing up the prayers in quiet confidence. For example

Be still and know that I am God . . .
He is Lord, he is Lord . . .

If you are praying for a particular part of the world, it can be
helpful to use some music from that area, as found in *World Praise*
(Marshall Pickering, 1993), or in two books of 'Songs from the
World Church' from the Wild Goose Worship Group: *Many and
Great* (1990) and *Sent by the Lord* (1991) or seasonal material from
Christian Aid, or USPG's *Let All the World*.

The address of Wild Goose Publications is Iona Community, Pearce
Institute, 840 Govan Road, Glasgow G51 3UU.

4 Meditation using a hymn or song at the beginning and end. There is often a great contrast between the way the hymn is sung ordinarily at the start, and very thoughtfully by the end. Alternatively, verses may be interleaved with prayers throughout. For example

When I survey the wondrous cross (see example following)
My song is love unknown (not all seven verses!)
Father we love you, we worship and adore you.

5 Prayers over 'secular' music can sometimes be helpful, but be aware of the danger of gimmickry, and the necessity of careful rehearsal to make sure the words fit the music in both mood and timing. Such prayers are usually more meditative than overtly intercessory, but can be appropriate to a particular theme. For example, Beethoven's 6th Symphony or the opening of Mahler's 2nd can be used for a service on creation.

Other useful music is very much a matter of individual taste and imagination, but here is a start:

Gabriel's theme from the film *The Mission* (available on cassette or CD) – an evocative oboe melody.

Vaughan Williams' 'The Lark Ascending' – an exquisite violin takes the spirit heavenwards.

Elton John's 'Song for Guy' (on *The Very Best of Elton John*) – a memorable instrumental piece.

Officium, by the Hilliard Ensemble with Jan Garbarek – an original and haunting blend of medieval chant and free-floating saxophone.

John Taverner's *The Protecting Veil* (opening).

Albinoni's *Adagio*.

Barber's *Adagio for Strings*.

Vaughan Williams' *Fantasia on a Theme* of Thomas Tallis.

6 Another excellent source of music for use in prayer is Decani Music, 30 North Terrace, Mildenhall, Suffolk IP28 7AB. They handle music from the St Thomas More Group. Note especially

Sing of the Lord's Goodness, God Beyond All Names, Songs of Hope. All these would greatly enrich the musical range of any church.

(33) WHEN I SURVEY THE WONDROUS CROSS

The following example of meditation through music is not strictly intercession. It is, however, prayer for oneself and shows the possibilities of using hymns and songs. The organist or music leader needs to have carefully rehearsed the musical entrances and be in possession of a full script. Alternatively, the words of the hymn can be said by the leader or by another voice.

SUNG   When I survey the wondrous Cross,
                 On which the Prince of glory died,
                 My richest gain I count but loss,
                 And pour contempt on all my pride.

Lord, usually we just 'see' the cross; we don't 'survey' it. We see it and take it for granted. But sometimes we truly catch a glimpse of the depth and tragedy of it, and our pride crumbles around us. This was the Prince of glory, the Lord of heaven, and we nailed him to earth. What total incomprehension! What sinful stupidity! Our richest gains – our petty ambitions, our greed for luxuries, our dream of the lottery jackpot – how small and mean they look. And our trivial pursuit of pride – how paltry! Lord, break the pride which seals us in our tombs; open our eyes to see what is truly valuable; help us to see all things in the light of the wondrous cross.

SUNG   Forbid it, Lord, that I should boast
                 Save in the Cross of Christ my God;
                 All the vain things that charm me most,
                 I sacrifice them to his Blood.

Lord, you know how we like to boast. We do it subtly. So people will notice, but not think we are boasting. It is pathetic really. The vain things that charm us most are nice clothes rather than a lovely character, foreign holidays rather than journeys of the spirit. As a nation, Lord, bring us to penitence, to our senses, to the cross; and there teach us with tender patience, to start again. Teach us that holiness exalts a nation, that justice is indivisible, that mercy is the common currency of your Kingdom. Teach us to start every journey, every day, at the holy, level ground at the foot of your cross.

SUNG   See from his head, his hands, his feet,
        Sorrow and love flow mingling down;
        Did e'er such love and sorrow meet,
        Or thorns compose so rich a crown?

Lord, on Golgotha we crucified Love. Your nature was love; your ways were love; your motive was love; your touch was love. And we crucified it. O reckless Love, that trusted itself to humanity! So from your head, your hands, your feet we see love poured out, mingled with divine sorrow at our blindness. And still you suffer for us, on your cross, until every man, woman and child has been brought to the place of sanity and starting again. Help us to point others to the love and sorrow of your cross. Let our evangelism be gentle, quiet even, but let it be steady and sure. And may many come to this church because they have seen the life, death and resurrection of Jesus, his love and sorrow, lived out in his people here.

SUNG   Were the whole realm of nature mine,
        That were an offering far too small;
        Love so amazing, so divine,
        Demands my soul, my life, my all.

What can we say? Your love renders us speechless. There is nothing we can put in the balance to deserve it. Perhaps we can at last stop trying to earn that love, and simply receive it. With simple, utter gratitude. Then we can start again — not earning, but offering; not deserving, but responding; wanting to let that love which we have received, flow on through us and into the lives of others. The hard, parched ground of this crazy world is waiting for the streams of love which the Church tentatively offers; waiting for them to grow into the full flood of your glory. Make us this week, wider channels of that love. Point us to those who need that love. Keep us always in that love. For, 'love so amazing, so divine, demands my soul, my life, my all'.

Repeat last verse: Were the whole realm of nature mine . . .

4 INTERCESSION IN ALL-AGE WORSHIP

PRACTICALITIES

EXAMPLES OF DIFFERENT METHODS

The growth in popularity of the All-age Service and the Family Service has raised sharply the issue of how prayer can be offered helpfully and effectively in this context. Much work has been done on talks, music and the structure of such services but much less on the central act of praying. In part this is because such services tend to be stronger on teaching and fellowship than on evoking a sense of the presence of God in a potentially lively atmosphere. The following ideas are an invitation to take more time and trouble over the important action of intercession in all-age worship.

PRACTICALITIES

1 Aim for participation. This is an interactive age when children and young people, and increasingly their parents, have been brought up with participatory forms of learning. With interactive computer learning in school and home, they will be increasingly involved in their own learning in the future. Listening to one person at the front is becoming a rare experience. In our intercessions, therefore, it is possible to expect a degree of involvement from the congregation, as is shown by many of the examples which follow. We need to be sensitive to the particular style and culture of our own church, however, and cannot assume that every congregation will find it easy.

2 Visual reinforcement. This is also an age of visual images, when what is seen is understood much more than what is merely heard. Without pandering completely to the sound bite and the flickering image, Christian communication needs to reckon with the seriousness of this cultural and perceptual change, even in prayer. One obvious opportunity this gives us is the use of the overhead projector (see later), but there are many other possibilities of demonstrating that a picture is worth a thousand words.

3 Beware of gimmicks. In the light of the above, the temptation might be to devise ever more sophisticated and clever tricks for prayer in all-age worship, in order to keep people's interest. However, this undermines the whole purpose of the exercise which is to help people take their heartfelt concerns to the loving mystery of God himself. We need to devise imaginative ways of prayer which offer a simple and genuine engagement with God. This is where the use of candles and other simple images such as hands, leaves, water, nuts etc. can be especially helpful.

4 Use appropriate vocabulary. The use of appropriate language is a continual snare for those who lead all-age worship. It may be too adult ('Let us confess our sins in penitence and faith, firmly resolved to keep God's commandments'), or too childish ('Let's say sorry for when we've been naughty'). Neither adults nor children want to be insulted. A good balance of language is a real art, learned by observation and practice. Language should also be concrete, about things rather than concepts. This does not mean that all metaphor, poetry and richness of language has to be avoided, rather that we should limit our flights of fancy.

5 Be brief. Several short prayers are better than a long, involved one. Each prayer should have a clear focus, and when we have finished we should stop speaking!

6 Pray about real issues in the wider world. Too easily all-age prayer can seem like a 'lowest common denominator' experience. It is safe to pray for parents, school, people who are ill, and the times we have been nasty to our friends. But prayer is also about touching the terror, pain and glory of creation and we sell people short if we domesticate the grandeur of the enterprise.

7 Aim for a balance of familiarity and variety. Repeating familiar actions is a favourite ploy of parents and teachers the world over. Games, stories, catchphrases can all be repeated seemingly endlessly. Adults, too, like a sense of security, of being in known territory with familiar routines, rituals and expectations. So it is often helpful to have ways of prayer which by their familiarity allow the congregation to settle quickly into the actual business of praying (see the following examples with candles). On the other hand, the appeal of the unexpected is another factor of human experience, and variety in prayer gives a new opportunity for it to become real (see the following 'Water into wine'). A balance is necessary, and a knowledge of what helps this particular unique congregation to pray most helpfully.

8 Don't embarrass people. Don't put people on the spot. Enough other people will usually volunteer to take part in the intercessions if they are invited warmly and confidently. On the other hand, if we are tentative and ponderous in our invitation, then we may experience difficulty in getting volunteers out to the front.

9 Don't be afraid of trying quiet moments in prayer. Children, even quite young ones, are often very responsive to moments of attentive silence. However, don't count on the atmosphere being right; it only needs one small child to have a noisy interlude for the whole adventure of silence to become impossible.

10 Be imaginative about leadership. It is good at some services to have a family or a group of mixed ages leading prayer, each in their own form of language. Organizations or church groups (youth groups, house groups) can well be asked to lead the prayers but we need to beware just asking, say, a uniformed organization to take the prayers without careful preparation. In certain churches it is possible to have people pray in small groups in the pews, but this requires care since people should not be embarrassed, and a newcomer could easily feel out of his or her depth.

RESPONSES AND LITANIES

Intercessions in all-age worship don't need to be novel or odd to be effective. However, they do need to be interesting and participatory. What follows is a series of simple intercession ideas based on response, rhythm or familiarity. The words here may not be appropriate to your situation, but the ideas themselves should be transferable to different times and places.

(34) RESPONSES – FOR ORDINARY PROBLEMS

Lord we bring to you today some of the ordinary, unspectacular things which have been happening around us this week, but which have affected people deeply.

We bring to you today all those who have been victims of crime this week, and feel angry or afraid.

Lord, in you we trust **we look to you for help**.

We bring to you today all those who have had major arguments this week and don't know how to get back to safety.

Lord, in you we trust **we look to you for help**.

We bring to you today all those who have had bad news this week, and don't know how they will cope.

Lord, in you we trust **we look to you for help**.

We bring to you today all those who have tried very hard to do something this week but have not been able to achieve it.

Lord, in you we trust **we look to you for help**.

We bring to you today our close family and best friends, and ask for your blessing on them, wherever they are, and whatever they need. Lord, in you we trust **we look to you for help**.

We bring to you today our own concerns, our hopes and fears, our plans and problems, and in a silent moment we tell you what they are and why they matter to us . . .

Lord, in you we trust **we look to you for help**.

(35) RESPONSES – FOR FAMOUS PEOPLE

We pray today for famous people, on whom much depends and of whom we expect much. We pray for sportsmen and women, big names and smaller ones, that they may give an example to younger people by the way they train and live and handle being famous.

Lord, we thank you **for hearing our prayers**.

We pray for TV and movie stars, today's favourites and those on the way up, that they may keep in touch with reality and use their fame and wealth for others as well as for themselves.

Lord, we thank you **for hearing our prayers**.

We pray for politicians and big businessmen and women, and people we see a lot in the news. May they remember that they are responsible to the rest of us, and also to you.

Lord, we thank you **for hearing our prayers**.

We pray for our own special heroes, the people we look up to and maybe want to be like. May they know your love and support, and never let themselves, or us, down.

Lord, we thank you **for hearing our prayers**.

We pray for ourselves, for we too are special to others, stars in their eyes; we pray that we may live up to the best that we are able, depending on your grace and strength.

Lord, we thank you **for hearing our prayers**.

(36) THE BEATITUDES

Lord we remember before you those who are struggling in life, and feel they haven't got enough strength inside them to cope.

Blessed are the poor in spirit
for theirs is the kingdom of heaven.

We remember before you those who have lost someone very special to them, and are wandering along the dark valley of bereavement.

Blessed are those who mourn **for they will be comforted**.

We remember before you those who deliberately choose not to push their way through life treading on other people, but try to live in a gentler, more generous way.

Blessed are the meek **for they will inherit the earth**.

We remember before you those who give their time and effort to important causes, to fight against hunger, torture, or the exploitation of our planet.

Blessed are those who hunger and thirst for righteousness
for they will be filled.

We remember before you those who turn their back on vengeance and bitterness, and so try to stop the cycles of destruction in our world, by showing the alternative way of Jesus.

Blessed are the merciful **for they will be shown mercy**.

We remember before you the people who inspire us to live better lives; those who have a love and a joy in them which make us ashamed, and determined to do better.

Blessed are the pure in heart **for they will see God**.

We remember before you those who both on the world stage and in ordinary living give themselves to the task of making peace a reality.

Blessed are the peacemakers
for they will be called the children of God.

We remember before you those who refuse to compromise on the truth, and are prepared to pay the price.

Blessed are those who are persecuted because of righteousness
for theirs is the kingdom of heaven.

And blessed are we all when people insult us and falsely say all kinds of things about us because of Jesus Christ.

Let us even rejoice and be glad, because great is our reward in heaven.

(37) CANDLES

The use of candle light to focus prayer is powerfully effective with most age groups. Silence for personal prayer is somewhat riskier, depending on local factors, but even young children can be responsive to the reflective atmosphere of candle light and quiet. This form of prayer is best in a fairly informal atmosphere but many all-age services could make use of the following example or variations of it.

What you need

- a table, display stand or equivalent
- a sand tray or multiple candle-holder
- candles and matches; night-lights are satisfactory but four-inch slim candles are more effective.

What to do

1 Ask people to think what or who they want to pray for – situations from the week's news, people they know in need, things happening in church or at school.

2 Ask the first person to come out to where the candles are, and to say what it is they want to pray for.

3 Have that person light their candle and place it in the sand or the candle-holder, saying 'We pray for . . .'.

4 Keep 15–20 seconds silence for people to pray.

5 Ask for another prayer request, and repeat as often as time or concentration allows.

6 Explain at the end that the candles will be left burning for the rest of the service as a reminder of our prayers, and of the fact that God does not forget but goes on working with our prayers after our thoughts have moved on.

Variation 1

The leader can invite the people to come out, name their concerns and light their candles, but leave the time of silent prayer until all the candles have been lit. Or instead of silence, the intercession leader can make a multiple prayer including all the situations which have been mentioned.

Variation 2

Have those who come out with the prayer requests remain out at the front holding their candle before them, forming in the end a strong visual reminder of our prayers. However, if this is to be done the candles will have to be in cardboard candle-holders to avoid candle-grease burns.

(38) LEAVES ON THE TREE

This prayer activity can be done in a variety of ways but a major difference is caused by the size of the congregation. It is based on the picture in Revelation 22 of the tree of life on which 'the leaves of the tree are for the healing of the nations'.

What you need

- a six-foot drawing of a tree with branches but no leaves
- a large number of paper 'leaves'
- felt-tip pens
- Blu-tack or equivalent.

What to do: smaller congregation

1 Explain about the tree of life. The leaves we put on our tree today represent our prayers for the healing of God's world and his people.

2 Give out a leaf and a pen to everyone (or have them already in or under the seats).

3 Ask people individually or with a friend or family member to write on the leaves some situations or people in need of God's healing.

4 Ask people when they are ready, to come out and put their leaves on the tree, quietly and reflectively, as a prayer. Stick-on substances should be available in small pieces by the tree.

5 Collect up all the 'leaf-prayers' in one final prayer.

What to do: larger congregation

1 Explain about the tree of life as above.

2 Ask people to think of places and people in need of God's healing. Ask for a volunteer to come out and to write their particular place or person on a leaf, having told the congregation about it first.

3 Stick the leaf on the tree. Repeat as often as necessary to build up a tree of prayer.

4 Collect up all the 'leaf-prayers' in one final prayer.

(39) CHRISTMAS PAPER-CHAIN

This prayer activity needs careful logistical planning. The equipment needs to be in the right place, and there need to be people around who know what is being planned and can act decisively at the right moment.

What you need

– a large number of individual strips for paper-chains
– a large number of pens.

What to do

1 Give out paper-chain strips and pens to everyone. Distribute through volunteers or have the materials already in the pews.

2 Invite everyone to write on one side of the strip of paper the names of the people with whom they will be spending Christmas Day, and on the other side, some special person or situation they want to pray for at Christmas time, such as the poor or lonely or homeless.

3 Explain that when we pray, we pray as a Church – altogether – and our strips of paper should therefore be

joined up and taken to God together. In that way we will be praying for each other at Christmas (one side of the paper) and for special needs (the other side).

4 Ask people to make chains out of their strips and their neighbours', and have your prearranged people do the joining up of short chains into longer and longer ones, until ideally one entire chain is produced. These people need to have a supply of blank strips to do the final joining.

5 The complete chain can be arranged in a significant place, e.g. around the altar, symbolizing the people of God, with their prayers, gathering around him. When it is in place a final joining prayer can be made, bringing all the individual prayers together.

(40) THE EMPTY TOMB

This activity is suitable for Easter Day and one or possibly two Sundays afterwards.

What you need

- an Easter garden which is reasonably easy for people to see
- pieces of paper and pens, either in the pews or ready to be given out by volunteers.

What to do

1 Introduce the intercessions by suggesting to people that the empty tomb reminds us of a God of surprises who does amazing things with the most unlikely situations.

2 Ask everyone to think of people who are in really hard places through illness or depression or unemployment or tragedy. Or situations which seem beyond hope – wars or minor conflicts which go on and on. Or personal needs which never seem to get any easier. This can be done in

pairs or family groups, as well as individually. If it is done in groups, people should be asked to turn to their neighbour or the couple of people nearest them. With confident encouragement and a sense of humour, they will do it!

3 Ask people to write these needs on the pieces of paper and have them collected up. Then take them to the Easter garden and put them outside the empty tomb, saying that we are taking our prayers here so that God might roll the stones away from the dark places, the 'tombs', which lie behind these prayers, and let his new life shine out.

4 Say a prayer such as:

> Easter God, in this wonderful festival we remember how the stone was rolled away from the tomb on that resurrection morning. The tomb was empty, death defeated, Jesus alive! We bring to you now some of the things which lie in a different kind of tomb, things which we worry about, which lie in dark places in our hearts and seem impossible. We ask you to roll away the stones from in front of these problems so that your Easter light may shine through. So may your will be done and your Kingdom come, for Jesus' sake. **Amen.**

(41) BRINGING PEOPLE TO THE CROSS

This form of intercession is clearly appropriate in a service which has the cross as a theme, but it can also be used more generally. In one sense, what we are always doing as we pray for people is bringing them to the cross where Christ showed his love for them and for all humanity. The image of the cross is always powerful, but this method of prayer would especially fit any all-age worship near Holy Week.

What you need

- as many pieces of A5 or A6 paper as there are people in the congregation who can write or draw

- ball-point pens, felt-tip pens or pencils as above, placed in readiness at the end of pews or under chairs
- an adequate number of large collection plates.

What to do

1 Invite the congregation to fold their piece of paper in half vertically, and then about one third of the way down horizontally. When the piece of paper is opened out again it should be marked in the shape of the cross.

2 Ask everyone to think of people they would like to bring to Jesus in prayer, and then to write their names or draw them in the four sections marked on the paper. Parents and older children can help younger ones with this. These are the people we are bringing to be around the cross of Christ, from which his love flows.

3 Have all the crosses collected up, folded or unfolded as people wish. They are then brought to the worship leader who prays over them all, perhaps like this:

> Lord Jesus Christ, we bring to you now all these people we know and care for. We bring them to your cross, because we know that from your cross flows forgiveness, healing and life. We ask you now to take each of these people and meet their need with your astonishing love. We ask it in your name. **Amen.**

Variation

You can be more specific in suggesting what kind of people they might pray for by asking the congregation, e.g.,

- to put in the top left corner a member of their family;
- in the top right, a particular friend;
- in the bottom left, someone they have heard of recently with problems to face, possibly someone in the news;

- in the bottom right, themselves, for they too are deeply loved by God.

(42) SUPPORTED BY THE SPIRIT

The following form of prayer is particularly appropriate for Pentecost or any service on the theme of the Holy Spirit. It requires a congregation that is prepared to let its hair down! However, it serves as a vivid reminder of one of the main activities of the Holy Spirit, that of supporting those who are open to such help.

What you need

- pieces of A5 size paper for each person
- a few people who know how to make paper planes.

What to do

1 Talk about the way the Holy Spirit is our invisible support, always with us, holding us up, inspiring us. We would achieve so much more in our faith if we could learn to 'sail in the Spirit' rather than try to fly by ourselves. Our prayer too would be more effective if we could trust in the Spirit of God rather than try to make him do what we want.

2 Invite people to write on their paper the names of those for whom they would like to pray – family, friends, those with special needs, those facing major decisions, those with big responsibilities, and so on.

3 Ask everyone to make a paper plane out of their piece of paper, demonstrating from the front how it is done and inviting the 'planted' experts to help.

4 When everyone seems more or less ready, remind the congregation of the work of the Holy Spirit in supporting and holding people up, unseen but ever present, just like the air which supports these paper planes if we fly them. Then prepare everyone to launch their planes towards the altar or focal point of the church as a symbolic prayer.

5 With the words 'Let's pray!' everyone launches their planes. The leader says a final gathering prayer, such as:

> Lord, we thank you for the power of the Spirit to support us and hold us, whatever we have to do or whatever we are facing. We know that what you do for us, you can also do for others. So take these our prayers and carry these people closer to your kingdom, for Jesus' sake. **Amen.**

(43) WATER INTO WINE

This form of intercession is specifically designed to accompany the reading in John 2 where Jesus turns six jars of water into copious quantities of wine. The idea is simple but can probably only be used once in any one church, for reasons which will become obvious.

What you need

- a table large enough for the following:
- a large glass bowl, full of water
- a large glass jug
- a pottery jug – with some concentrate blackcurrant drink at the bottom
- a small (2-inch) glass.

What to do

1 Remind the congregation that Jesus took ordinary water and turned it into something extraordinary. We are going to pray that Jesus will take the ordinary concerns that we want to pray about and turn them into his extraordinary answers.

2 Invite people to think of those things which are on their hearts – people in trouble, places in the news, needs in the

church – and to come up to the table where the water and the jugs are. There they are invited to say what their concern is and to scoop some water out of the bowl with the small glass, and pour it into the pottery jug, as an act of prayer.

3 This is repeated as long as seems appropriate. The leader then reminds people that these are the prayers of the church this morning, brought to Jesus. The leader prays a comprehensive prayer, such as:

> Lord Jesus, we bring to you now all these our prayers. We add to them all the other unspoken concerns and prayers of the rest of us in church today. As in Cana you took the water and turned it into rich wine, so we ask you to take our ordinary prayers and turn them into your extraordinary answers, as is best in each situation. **Amen.**

4 The denouement comes when you now pour the water from the pottery jug (now of course turned a deep red), into the clear glass jug. Not a very clever trick, but effective nonetheless! End with a final word about never underestimating the power of God to answer our prayers.

(44) IN THE PALM OF GOD'S HANDS

This form of intercession is especially meant for praying for individuals. The basic idea, however, is capable of several variations and it is therefore a method which can be used on a number of occasions – though not too close together.

What you need

- a carved pair of hands – pottery, wood, china. Alternatively, a pair of hands can be made by someone with reasonable creativity; for example, from papier mâché.
- small pieces of paper and pens.

What to do

1 Place the carved hands in a visible place as the focus for the time of prayer, with the paper and pens nearby.

2 Read out Isaiah 49.15, 16, ending, 'I have carved you on the palm of my hands'. Talk about the lovely image of being held and nurtured by God, as a mother her child.

3 Invite the congregation to think of those people who especially need our prayers today – statesmen and women with great matters to decide, people in the news, people with decisions to make, friends who are ill, etc.

4 Invite people to come up and say who they want to pray for and why, and then to write that name on one of the pieces of paper and place it in the hands, representing the hands of God.

5 After a while, ask the congregation in their imagination to place the names they have thought of but which have not been mentioned, into the carved hands. Pick up the hands and offer them to God in a gathering prayer.

> Lord, we thank you for all these people, made and loved by you. You know their needs better than we do, and you also care for them even more than we do. They are carved in the palm of your hands. Take our prayers, we ask you, and use them to help bring about the things that are best for them. Keep us faithful in praying regularly for them, and doing whatever we can. For Jesus' sake. **Amen.**

Variation 1

Prayer can be made for anything by this method. The leader can ask for one or two prayers from each of a number of categories, e.g. the Church, the world, the community, the sick.

Variation 2

Give everyone a piece of paper and pen and have them write the names of the people they want to pray for. If the congregation is small, they should all have the chance to bring up their prayer at the end, or, in a Communion service, they could place the prayer in the hands as they go past to the Communion rail.

(45) STREET SCENES

One of the perennial tasks of teaching about prayer is to make it engage with everyday life and not be seen as an esoteric activity to do with vague and distant problems. The following is a straight challenge to the latter kind of prayer, but it needs the leader to be confident of his or her ability to handle quirky ideas quickly!

What to do

1 Remind the congregation that prayer is concerned with the real world because God is concerned with it too – he made it! Remind them also that we are told by Paul to 'pray constantly', not just in church, nor just in our special prayer time, but also as we go about our daily life. At any time we can bring any situation before God, and know that he will be concerned about it.

2 Ask for two volunteers to do something a bit different. Some fun can be had here but essentially all you are asking the two children to do (it will probably be children who volunteer, and older ones are best) is to go outside to the road by the church and notice everything that is going on. Give them two or three minutes to observe and remember, and then to come back.

3 When they are out, there is the chance to say a bit more about praying through the day. Why not pray about the news, even as you are watching it on TV? You can easily pray for people you pass in the street who look to be

carrying a heavy burden on their shoulders. What about sometimes taking a newspaper into your prayers? How often do you pray about your work and colleagues there, or your school and your friends?

4 When the two return, quiz them about what they have seen – the cars, the children running by, the advertising hoardings, the cat asleep on the wall, the teenager with the ghetto-blaster. Then try to turn these observations into prayer – the difficult bit! The prayer should be meditative and not rushed, sincere rather than grammatically polished. It should demonstrate how ordinary events in life are often openings to prayer.

For example:

– pray for those who are *driving* long distances today, and those who have newly started driving.
– pray for the *children* of this neighbourhood, their parents and schools, for good role models in their parents and teachers.
– pray for those who work in the *advertising* industry, for integrity and a framework of values; and for us as consumers, that we should ask the right questions.
– pray for our respect for all God's creation, *cats* included! But especially for a wise preservation of all that is becoming scarce in nature.

5 Introduce the Lord's prayer, saying that in it Jesus taught us to pray that God's Kingdom would come on earth itself, not just in heaven.

(46) CELTIC CIRCLING PRAYER

The renewal of interest in Celtic spirituality has opened up a wealth of images and shapes of prayer for the contemporary Church. One of the most characteristic features of Celtic prayer is the idea of enfolding or circling; this is the basis of the following method of intercession.

123

What to do

1 Explain to the congregation that Celtic prayer was a very ancient and distinctively British form of Christian prayer and had particular emphases. One was the idea of enfolding or circling loved ones in God. A similar biblical picture for this is found in Psalm 34.7: 'The angel of the Lord encamps around those who fear him, and he delivers them.' The Celtic word was the *caim*; they drew a circle around themselves and their loved ones, and it was called a *caim*. Sometimes they would actually point their finger and draw it around themselves.

2 Say that first of all we are going to draw the *caim* around the congregation here this morning. Ask for two volunteers and take them with you as you circle the congregation, walking around slowly and talking about the need for God's protection around us in times of vulnerability – which come often! When you have returned to the front of the people, pray for God's protection around everyone this week, or use a Celtic prayer from one of the popular collections which now exist, for example, David Adam's *Tides and Seasons* (Triangle, 1989).

3 Now ask people to close their eyes and imagine their own family or special people standing together. Invite them in their imagination to draw the *caim* around that group, slowly and deliberately. Then offer the same, or another prayer, for God's protection, strength and love.

4 Now invite people to draw the *caim* around themselves, and to picture themselves within the circle of God's loving care. In that security invite them to mention to God any need that occupies their minds, anything that worries them, anything that makes them feel insecure. Then offer the same, or another prayer.

5 Perhaps end with the following:

The breadth of God enfold us
The depth of God uphold us

The love of Christ surround us
The joy of Christ around us

Spirit's life give peace to us
Spirit's fire increase in us

Holy Three in you we rest
Now, tomorrow, ever blessed.

(47) PRAYING ROUND THE CHURCH

One of the best aids to prayer we have is the church building, which often is full of features which can be used to trigger prayer. I have assumed in the following a traditional parish church. Modern school halls may provide more of a challenge.

What to do

1 Ask for volunteers to go on a prayer walk around the church. Take a reasonable number and set off for the front. Have a conversation with the children you have gathered, about what happens here. Then pray for what it represents, perhaps starting like this:

> Lord, we pray for those who have been baptized here
> recently, remembering . . .
> we pray for those in this and other countries who
> have recently come to faith . . .
> we pray for all the children born this week in our
> neighbourhood . . .

2 Move off to the pulpit. Ask the children what happens here, and what the preacher talks about. Then pray, starting with phrases such as these:

> Lord, we pray for all the thousands of men and women
> all over the country who are preaching today . . .
> we pray that the preaching in this church may be
> faithful and effective . . .
> we pray that we may be good and active listeners
> to your word . . .

3 Move off to the altar or Communion table and have a question and answer conversation with the children. Then pray, perhaps with these ideas:

> Lord, we pray that this may be a place of unity amongst
> Christians . . .
> we pray that as we come here week by week we
> may meet you in deeper and richer ways . . .
> we pray that the world may be fed both physically
> and spiritually . . .

4 All sorts of other places could be used: the door – as a place to pray for the outreach of the church; the windows – as a place to pray for the light of Christ to pour into the church's life; the bookstall – as a place to pray for countries where it is hard to get hold of Christian literature, and that the congregation may buy and benefit from such books.

Variation

Displays about various aspects of the church's life can be spread around the church and people asked to go from one display to another, silently praying at each. To do this in a more orderly way, music can be played as the cue to move on, e.g., 'We are praying in the love of God, we are praying in the love of God' to the tune 'We are walking in the light of God'.

(48) RINGING THE BELL

In many faiths the ringing of a bell has special significance. It marks a special moment and focuses the mind and heart. In the following intercession this time-honoured ritual has the added value of allowing active participation in the making of prayer.

What you need

A handbell or a gong, suitably visible to the congregation. If a gong is to be used the leader would have to be sure that the Eastern mystical associations would not create too many difficulties for the particular congregation.

What to do

1 By question and answer draw out the significance of bells in worship. Bells call the faithful to worship, they are used to celebrate a wedding or, muffled, to mark a death. In some churches they are rung when the bread and wine at Communion is held up by the priest. What is the common theme? Answer: the ringing of a bell marks a special moment.

2 Explain that what you are going to do today is ask people, if they want, to come out to the bell (or even better, the gong), to say what they want to pray for, to ring the bell and then keep a moment's quiet as the prayer is received by God.

3 Suggest some of the broad categories for which people might want to pray, e.g., items in the news, friends in need, events to celebrate, long-term problems in the world. Invite people to come out, say what they want to pray for, ring the bell or strike the gong, and wait.

4 Encourage everyone to honour the quiet moment after the bell has been rung. With a gong especially there can be a

rich resonance which dies gently away (the prayer being taken into the heart of God). This can be a precious moment of attentiveness.

5 Continue as appropriate, and perhaps end yourself with a number of rings for those items you judge have been missed out. Finish with a prayer.

> Lord, we believe that these our prayers are ringing in the halls of heaven. Thank you for hearing them, although we know that you will also hear the merest whisper of our hearts. Send, we pray, your sure answers, so that our lives may ring with your praise. **Amen.**

(49) USING AN OHP

The overhead projector is a stock-in-trade of many churches today. Some are less happy about using it in worship than in the youth group, but its flexibility and clarity have made it much used in all-age worship, especially for the lyrics of songs. Here is an obvious extension of its use.

What to do

1 Ask the congregation what is on their minds from the week's news. As items are mentioned they are noted down as one- or two-word topics for prayer on the OHP. A gathering prayer can then be said by you as the leader, or a set prayer for the needs of the world can be read by a child.

2 Then ask the congregation what we should be praying for this morning for the Church, both locally and more widely. A similar process of writing up and praying should follow. Repeat with prayer for individuals. A new acetate should be used for each main division of prayers, and the writing should be large, bold and colourful.

3 A final acetate should be put up with a picture of a symbol of stillness on it (candle, praying hands, cross) or a single

word (Jesus, Lord, Abba). Invite people to make their own silent prayer for themselves, for their needs too are of concern to God.

4 End with a final prayer, perhaps one with a little more formality from a recognized service book, to round off the intercessions.

Variation

Headlines and photos from the week's newspapers can be cut out, stuck on to white paper and then photocopied on to the special acetates designed for copiers. (Do not attempt to use ordinary ones, which make a sticky mess inside the copier.) These cuttings make the link with the real needs of the world even more vividly than memory. The sheets should then be displayed with time for a leader's prayer, spontaneous prayer from the congregation, or silence, whichever is most appropriate to the particular congregation and occasion.

5 INTERCESSION IN SMALL GROUPS

Near the spiritual heart of many churches are the small groups which meet regularly to uphold the whole life of the church in prayer. They may be House Groups, Praise and Prayer groups, Julian meetings for silent prayer, the Mothers' Union prayer group, the Ministry Team meeting or any other of a hundred forms of the church prayer group. Each usually settles into a routine of praying which works for them, but the possibility is real that members are longing for a change, for something to freshen up their ways of prayer. It is also possible that people do not come to the group because they suspect it of being rather dry and dusty. And yet we know that prayer is a sacred duty resting on the Christian and that the future of the Church and the world somehow depend on it. The stakes are high. What follows are some further ways of praying in small groups which might be of help. Best of all, they might stimulate new ideas in the reader him- or herself.

PRACTICALITIES

1 Establish clear boundaries. A prayer group may handle some very personal issues both of the members and of people who have given their permission for their situation to be prayed for. Boundaries of confidentiality should be clear and brought up in a conscious way, not simply trusting to the good sense and Christian virtue of the group. People are often not aware of the damage that can be done to others until it is too late.

2 Establish a clear understanding of what the shape of the time of prayer will be. The leader of the session will need to make sure that everyone understands what is going to happen, so that they can relax into it and participate. Equally they need to know what is expected of them, and that they do not need to participate actively if they do not wish to. The question should be asked: 'Is everyone comfortable with that?'

3 Beware of the cringe factor. Some people inwardly crawl into a hole when asked to do different things in a group. The extrovert leader may have no idea what such people are going through. New ideas should therefore be introduced slowly and carefully.

4 Make sure that the method is not too artificial or too introverted. The method used should not be more important than the primary purpose, which is to pray. When the style of prayer has become the focus of attention rather than holding together God's goodness and our needs, then it has come off the tracks. For example, a complex activity to decide what should be prayed for, or an over-long congregational response, can distract people from actually praying. Equally, we must be careful not to let the prayer become too introspective and 'churchy'. The temptation to 'spiritual gossip' in such groups is strong, and there is a world outside awaiting our work of loving prayer.

5 Give opportunity to review the form of prayer used. One of the great values of group prayer is that there is an opportunity to learn what helped and why, what hindered and how it could be avoided another time, and so on. We learn a lot about prayer from listening to others talk about it, and the shared experience of an actual time of prayer can provide real opportunity to grow in this way. It also gives people a chance to off-load particular problems they may have had with that experience and so prevents them going away frustrated and annoyed. A simple question is enough: 'So what was helpful, and what wasn't, with that way of praying?'

6 Don't forget that the normal processes of group life are still taking place. Just because the task of this group is prayer, it doesn't mean that normal group-process is interrupted. There will still be factors of lay-out, comfort and lighting to see to. Prayer is not the only task: there is the task of group maintenance and the needs of individual members to consider as well. There may still be the problem of the dominant speaker, the attention-seeker, the hidden conflict, even spiritual competition. The leader has to be attentive in many directions at once.

(50) A STANDARD WAY OF PRAYING TOGETHER

Before looking at other, more unusual ways of praying in groups it is worth simply finding a bench-mark of good standard practice which has worked in a variety of forms for many years in many places. It is always good to have a safe place to come home to.

What to do

1 Start by sharing news of each other and of the church. This is the stuff of fellowship, but also of prayer. It can be done with more sense of purpose if the leader invites each person – if they wish – to tell the group some of the highs and lows of their week.

2 The group can then be asked what they would like to pray about particularly on this occasion. This time needs to be kept under control or it becomes all talk and little prayer.

3 One person can then give a 'thought for the day', read a passage from the Bible or another book, give a short talk on a Bible passage – whatever is within the capacity and inclination of the individual and the group. What is happening is that something outside the concerns and problems so far identified by the group is being brought into it, so that there is something else to chew on. In the strange economy of the Holy Spirit this 'something else' will often prove relevant to the later time of prayer.

4 This time of prayer now begins. It may helpfully be broken up into sections, e.g., (i) thanksgiving, (ii) prayer for wider issues, (iii) prayer for the local church and for individuals. People should be encouraged to be brief and not to worry about sentence construction. In the thanksgiving period in particular, short phrases are ideal, and nothing is too small to be a cause of gratitude. People should also be reassured that silence is not a problem but an opportunity for silent prayer, deeper reflection, and for other issues to break through to the surface which might otherwise have remained hidden. Five to ten minutes may be enough for each section, but that very much depends on the nature of the group. Some might make a night of it!

5 The leader will have been moving the process along and now has to bring it to an end. One way is openly to recognize that there are many other prayers which could have been said, and so to offer all our spoken and unspoken prayers to God. Then finish with a more formal prayer which gathers up the whole process in thanksgiving and trust.

Variations

There can be any number of variations on this process. Music, sung or listened to, is a good lead-in or conclusion. A teaching tape might be used instead of local input. More order might be put into the prayer by using cycles of prayer or a map of the parish. Focus can be added by praying more extensively for Christian workers abroad with whom the church is linked. Prayer is as varied as the people who pray.

(51) THE VASE

This is a simple but effective way of praying for others (or of giving thanks). It doesn't depend on verbal dexterity but on the careful building up of the corporate prayer of the group. Eventually this prayer becomes a thing with its own beauty.

What you need

- a simple but stable vase
- a collection of flowers and greenery which will fit into the vase.

What to do

1 Place the vase on a low table in the middle of the group, with the flowers and greenery alongside it.

2 Invite people to come forward when they have something to pray for, and to say what the concern is as they place the flower in the vase. It may be enough simply to say 'For X who is starting a new job . . .', or 'Please pray for Y to know God's peace'.

3 The activity continues in prayerful silence until all who want have contributed their concern and is then closed in vocal prayer by the leader.

(52) PRAYING IN PAIRS

In a group that has relaxed, and where people have grown to trust each other, this approach can provide deep mutual support. In a newer or more formal group it will probably prove too intense at first.

What to do

1 Divide the group up into pairs and invite one to tell the other about the pressure points of their lives at present, or the issues they are facing. The other should then pray, naturally and straightforwardly, for the person, allowing silence to listen to God and to let the Spirit pray within him or her (Romans 8.26). After the initial five minutes clarifying the nature of the need, what follows should be prayer and not further discussion.

2 Reverse the process, allowing perhaps twenty minutes for the whole experience.

3 Encourage members of the group to continue to pray for their partner during the week, but to be aware of the need for confidentiality.

(53) CANDLE POWER

There are many variations on the use of candles for intercession. Night-lights can be bought cheaply; four-inch slim candles look better but are harder to keep safe from dripping wax. A slightly darkened room can contribute to the powerful atmosphere engendered by the light, reminding us of the light that shines in the darkness, but which the darkness has never put out (John 1.5).

What you need

– an appropriate number of suitable candles, with matches and a taper
– a sand tray or protected table.

What to do (with night-lights)

1 Before the start of the group meeting, arrange the night-lights in the shape of a cross or a circle, with a larger candle within it.

2 Start the time of intercession with the lighting of the larger candle and suitable words: e.g., Jesus said: 'I am the light of the world: whoever comes to me will not walk in darkness but will have the light of life.'

3 Invite group members to name situations and people in need of the light of Christ, and as they name them, to come up and light a candle from the larger candle with a taper. Time for silent prayer for that concern should be left, and then another group member could come up. In the end there will be a pool of light, which remains as a sign of hope until the end of the session.

4 The leader reads further suitable passages, e.g., 'You are the light of the world . . .' (Matthew 5.14–16), and closes with prayer.

Variation 1

If night-lights are not used, each person can be given a candle (with a protective holder), with which they can come forward and light from the one central candle as they name their prayer-concern. The result is a ring of light rather than a pool.

Variation 2

A single candle is lit from the large central one. The first person, while holding the candle, prays that the light of Christ may shine in the life of someone, or the darkness of some situation, according to what is on their heart. That person then passes it on to the next person, who does the same, or sits with it in silent prayer before passing it on again. And so on around the group.

(54) RESTING AND LIFTING

Intercession often seems to be a great effort, and not very rewarding at the time. This activity for a group tries to take the 'work' out of it and to see intercession as simply lifting people and situations to God, as we rest safely in him.

What to do

Lead the group in words like these, and don't rush!

We're going to relax now in the presence of God ... let go of anxiety and stress ... be aware of tension in the body and let it go ... let God's love support you ... rest in it ... float in it ...

Now lift up to God anyone who is particularly on your mind ... lift them into the presence of God ... let them bask in his love ... let his healing love warm them through and through ...

One by one, lift up your special people into the presence and peace of God ... let them be surrounded by his goodness ... let his love work deeply within them ...

Now return to your own needs and rest in God's love again yourself ... be aware of his strength flooding into you ... restoring you, filling you ...

Turn now to larger problems, the things in this country that seem to be in deep need ... the anguish of other countries facing turmoil ... the pressures on the United Nations ... lift these up to God as well ... let his love envelop them ... his power transform them ...

See this damaged planet, struggling on with pollution, depleted forests and a damaged ozone layer ... and see this world, too, held in the embrace of its Creator ... loved and sustained ... renewed and healed ...

Now come back to rest in God's love again . . . let his strength fill
you . . . his presence around you and within you . . . the joy of the
Lord . . .

Now rest quietly in his presence, and wait . . . let the Spirit be your
guide, and bring to mind anything else for you to lift to God . . .

Now be aware of the group here in this room with you . . . and lift
them into God's healing, loving presence . . . that we may be one
. . . one with the Father . . . one in faith and hope and love . . .

May the love of the Father sustain us,
the joy of the Son en-trance us,
the power of the Spirit enliven us
and keep us in prayer for the world, now and always.

(55) STONES

*Small stones can be used powerfully in a number of ways. Preferably they
should be clean! Like hazel nuts and other small, natural objects they have
value in being easy to come by, and always being entirely unique. Their
value in the following intercession also lies in their hard and
uncompromising nature.*

What you need

- a number of small, clean stones
- a small standing cross 15–30 cms high.

What to do

1 Give out the stones by handing round a bowl from which
   the group members can select their own.

2 Invite the group to feel the unique contours of their own
   stone and to recognize its unyielding nature. Then ask

members to identify the stone with a hard problem they themselves, or someone they know, is facing. Reflect on the obdurate nature of the problem.

3 Then invite the group to come up one at a time, and, only when they are ready, to place the stone at the foot of the cross, and there to pray silently or aloud for Christ to redeem the situation, as he potentially redeemed all ills on the cross.

4 Conclude with a prayer, collect, reading or music, as fits the group.

Variation 1

The stones can be used to symbolize a sin or failure which is particularly resistant to change. Bringing it to the cross (silently) can be a more focused means of confession than is usual, and may give more meaning to the penitence.

Variation 2

Slightly larger stones can be used to symbolize the various elements of a project for which the group is praying. Being larger, the stones can be made to interlock and so create a cairn of faith and hope in which everybody's contribution is important. This can also be a symbol that the path ahead towards the completion of the project is being marked by prayer, as a cairn marks the path in exposed country.

(56) AN IMAGINATION WALK

This style of intercession is riskier but is guaranteed to help a number of people. It will also probably leave some people cold! It needs to offer genuine space for people to pray, and therefore the temptation for leaders to go through it too fast must be resisted. If people are not able to loiter as they walk, to see and hear the sights and sounds, they will not be able to pray. The leader should practise carefully, out loud, and try to adopt a neutral style which does not attract attention to herself. The congregation must be prepared by the leader explaining what is going to happen.

In these intercessions we are not going to pray in the usual way but we are going to go for a walk in our imagination. My words will move us on in our walk but they will be inviting you to pray for the familiar people and places in your life, so the praying is up to you. Just use your imagination . . .

Let's set off. Imagine that you are just stepping out of your home and looking around you at the familiar sights . . . houses, flats, parks, fields, places where your neighbours live . . . and where they have their dreams and their fears . . . people who hurry past with eyes on the pavement . . . people who smile shyly but don't give a lot away . . . ordinary people, sad people, excited people, anxious people . . . pray for them – your neighbours . . .

Now in your imagination set off walking down the road, passing the houses where you have friends . . . pray for them as you pass . . . remember their needs, their celebrations . . . walk on until you get to the shops, and watch the people scurrying in and out . . . so much to do, so serious . . . notice the harassed mother with her children . . . pray for her . . . notice the old man looking slightly bewildered . . . pray for him . . . pray for those who have to watch every penny, whose poverty is mocked by the bulging variety on the shelves . . . pray for anyone you know who quietly struggles to make ends meet . . .

Carry on walking, and in your imagination come to a place where people work, an office, a bank, a factory, and walk more slowly here . . . this is where people are fulfilled, earn their money, stretch their skills, meet their friends . . . or it is where people are trapped and trodden on, frustrated and bored . . . pray for the people who work there . . . see God's love there, his encouragement and generosity . . . and remember also the thousands of people who desperately want a job, and have sent in scores of applications, and are miserable and demoralized . . . pray for them . . . and anyone you know who has been made redundant . . .

Walk on past a school, and see the energy of the children and listen to the excited voices, full of life and hope . . . give thanks for the children . . . pray for the children who feel alone or frightened . . . pray for the teachers, for patience, imagination, enthusiasm, eyes to notice those who are struggling . . . hold this whole place in the warmth of God's love.

Walk on, and pray for those you pass . . . ask for the touch of Christ on each person . . . and then look up and see a church . . . on it a cross, symbol of a God who loved his world so much that he gave his only Son . . . loved the world, all of it . . . loved the people, all of them.

Let us pray for the Church and for the world, and let us thank God for his goodness. All week. Everywhere. **Amen.**

(57) NEWSPAPERS

A simple way of relating our praying to the stuff of everyday existence is to bring some of the day's papers to the group. Having to construct prayers out of concrete situations instead of general themes makes praying much more demanding, but also much more satisfying.

What to do

1   Give a daily paper to each group of three people. They can then take different pages in order to identify the stories they want to bring forward for prayer.

2   The small group discusses how they want to pray for a particular situation. For example: how bold or specific to be; what they really want to pray about in a case of child abuse; who to pray for in a case of fraud; does sport need prayer?

141

3 The group comes together after 10 to 15 minutes to offer the actual prayer. Each time, the headlines or first paragraph is read out at the start, followed by the form of prayer which the small group has decided is appropriate.

4 At the end the leader gathers the scattered parts of the newspaper, places them in the centre of the group and offers a collecting-up prayer. The newspaper has thus been 'broken open' under the love and judgement of God, and the news should probably feel rather different to members of the group throughout the rest of the week.

(58) HOLDING ON TO THE CROSS

This is a way of helping a group to pray for each other, but it runs the risk of embarrassment. Leaders will have to judge the appropriateness of the exercise.

What to do

A small cross is given to the first member of the group. As she holds it she briefly says what particular concerns she would like prayed for, if any. She has the option of passing the cross on to the next person. Members of the group pray silently or aloud for that person as long as she holds the cross. When she is ready, she passes the cross on, and the process is repeated.

(59) PICTURES . . .

The visual stimulus to prayer can be a great liberation to people who have only thought of words and concepts. This kind of activity is best done in a thoughtful group, not afraid to think out loud. Young people's groups often respond well to this exercise in prayer, as do home groups where members have relaxed with each other.

What to do

1 Collect a series of photographs from magazines, newspapers, etc. which tell a vivid story about places or situations of real human significance: e.g., violent scenes of protest, a family in poverty, a politician meeting the people, a graveyard, a 'For Sale' sign.

2 Have the group study the pictures carefully, brainstorming their responses to each of them, seeing what thoughts and feelings they evoke, asking them to look deeper into each picture than they would usually do. The importance of this is that people often have very different responses to the same picture, and we would not normally realize that this is the case when we see an image.

3 Ask the group how they would pray about each of the pictures and what they represent. Allow the group to discuss the appropriateness of each approach to prayer. Ask the question 'Does that kind of prayer do justice to the complexity of the situation?'

4 Move into a time of open prayer, bringing the different pictures into the centre of the group one at a time. Prayer is best done with eyes open on this occasion.

Variation

You can bring that day's newspapers to the group and ask them to reflect on the pictures of that day's news. Again, this sharpens up the adequacy and appropriateness of particular forms of prayer.

(60) . . . AND SLIDES

What to do

1 Set the group the task of preparing next Sunday's intercessions at church, using the slides which you have

taken yourself, or have got from someone else, or have picked up from your local Christian Resources Centre (many Anglican dioceses have them). The slides might be of contemporary scenes from today's culture, computers, money markets, the media, fashion, sport, entertainment, and so on; and pictures of the earth (from space), riots, armaments, poverty, forests and fields of grain; together with pictures of the cross, a church in the bush, a great cathedral, bread and wine, social work in a city, and so forth. A set of images of Christ as seen by artists in different cultures and in different periods of history can be an excellent resource.

2 You could offer the group some music which would enhance the effectiveness of the prayers. The range of possible music could include classical and popular music, evocative film themes or distinctively Christian music. The combination of slides, words and music make this an extremely complex task, but one which will generate concentration, thoughtfulness and a real appreciation of the importance and difficulty of intercession.

3 The group should not be large. Not very many people can get closely involved in such a detailed project. They should be given the task and then advised that a good approach is quickly to acquaint themselves with the slides and music available, and then to decide on a clear and simple theme, and the sort of structure they would like to use. Only then should they get down to detailed work in choosing slides and music and how they go together.

4 Aim for fewer slides with powerful images rather than sheer quantity. Give space for meditation. Give positive images, not just negative ones. Remember the potential of interspersing slides from, for example, Zeffirelli's television film *Jesus of Nazareth*, with scenes of everyday life in contemporary society.

5 The sheer practicalities of using slides in worship can negate the best-laid plans. All the details of projection, sound

amplification, timing, black-out, introductions and endings should be tried out in the actual place of worship. One of the best occasions for this kind of prayer is on a church weekend away where everyone is involved in preparing the final act of worship.

6 It may sound daunting but it is worth the risk. Some wonderfully evocative visual prayers and meditations will almost undoubtedly emerge.

(61) PRAYER AND PIZZA

This form of prayer might appeal to a youth group or a group which enjoys flexibility and fun. It has the benefits of being highly participatory, and of holding together two important appetites – for food and for prayer!

What you need

– a house with a large kitchen and a fair amount of oven space
– file cards or photocopies of a number of classic prayers.

What to do

1 At the previous meeting make sure everyone knows that they are being asked to come to a particular house with a favourite kind of pizza and a favourite prayer.

2 Have fun eating first, it's just a party! Then remind everyone that they are supposed to have brought a prayer but if anyone has forgotten or could not find a prayer, they can choose one of the prayers you have provided and which you have left lying around on cards for people to look at.

3 At a given moment have the group sit down and then ask people to say what prayer they have brought and why, before they actually pray it. Add one or two of your own.

145

General discussion may follow on what makes a prayer a 'classic', or on what moves us particularly in prayer.

4 The evening can end with open prayer, or with one of the prayers with which the group has especially identified.

(62) TAKING CHRIST INTO THE HOME

This is a form of guided meditation which is capable of much variation. It is a way of praying for the family, or the occupants of a house, or for oneself, and should be prepared with particular situations in mind. The leader should have the confidence not to go too fast, and should if possible have the kind of voice which is easy to listen to and is not intrusive. The leader explains that she is going to lead the group on an imaginative journey with Christ; they should go with it as much as they can but not worry if they can't get into it. There will be times of silence and times of moving on, and the whole experience will take about 10–15 minutes.

Imagine that you are standing outside your house, looking at its familiar features, and thinking of those who live in there . . . be aware that standing next to you is our Lord – however you want to imagine him . . . perhaps it is difficult to 'see' him . . . it doesn't matter . . . he's there, and he's with you; he's always on your side . . .

Take him now into your home . . . through the front door . . . what do you see? . . . who is around in the house? . . . go to the first person you see, in whatever room they are, and introduce Jesus to them . . . see what he does . . . be aware of the atmosphere . . . does Jesus speak? reach out a hand? what does he do? . . .

Then take Jesus on to meet the other people in your house . . . and watch him meeting them . . . see how people respond . . .

Now take him up to your own room, your special room, a room with large boxes around the shelves, each one representing an area of your life . . . what are the boxes called? . . . what do you look like? . . . are some bigger and heavier than others? . . . now take a box down . . . which one? . . . and let Jesus look into it . . . what does he do? . . . how do you feel? . . . what do you want to say to him? . . . and what does he say to you?

Now let him choose a box and look through it . . . does that feel OK? . . . again, what does he do? . . . and say? . . . perhaps you want to sit down and really talk with him . . . go ahead . . . *longer pause* . . .

The time comes to leave . . . how do those boxes look and feel now? . . . go downstairs again, and gather all the members of your house together . . . and let Jesus bless you . . . and the house . . . and then let him go . . .

Now come back here to this room, quietly, gently, in your own time . . . be aware of the ordinary features of this room, your chair, your body . . . we're back.

(63) THE WORLD MAP

It is often difficult to bring our prayer alive when we are remembering the world's needs and troubles. We tend to roll out the same list of generalizations. Here is a method of enabling a group to pray more vividly and specifically.

What you need

- a large wall map of the world
- about 20 night-lights
- a larger white candle.

What to do

1 Lay out the map on the floor with the night-lights arranged around the edges and the large candle at one corner.

147

2 Light the candles while saying (or having another person read) some of the New Testament references to light:

'I am the light of the world.' (John 9.5)
'Light has come into the world but people loved darkness rather than light.' (John 3.19)
'The light shines in the darkness and the darkness has never put it out.' (John 1.5)

3 Invite members of the group to think of those places in the world for which they have a special concern, either because they know someone living and working there, or because it is in the news, or because they have a long-term commitment to it. These are the places where we want the light of Christ to shine.

4 Then invite people to come forward one at a time, pick up a night-light and place it on the appropriate place on the map. Then they can say why they want to pray for that place, and either offer the prayer themselves, or leave space for quiet prayer, perhaps ending 'Lord, in your mercy **hear our prayer.'**

5 When the time is up, if there are candles still left, the leader should place them on other uncovered places, giving appropriate reasons, and then place the single larger candle firmly in the middle of the map, gathering up all the group's prayers and saying something like this:

God our Father, we thank you for the diversity of peoples and cultures all over the world. Thank you for the way you never leave yourself without witness in any part of your creation. Take our prayers now, and use them to bring about your purposes, so that the light of Christ may shine, and the kingdoms of this world become the Kingdom of our God and of his Christ, in whose name we ask it. **Amen.**

6 INTERCESSION IN PERSONAL PRAYER

Intercession for other people is often all that people think prayer is. Later they might see that intercession is just the tip of the iceberg, but the enormous significance of it remains a true insight. Unfortunately this is also the area where many Christians find their praying coming unstuck. It seems full of duty and boredom, and their failure to pray adequately (as they see it) leaves a residue of guilt. What follows are some different ways of engaging in personal intercession which might breathe life and hope into the privilege of praying for others.

PRACTICALITIES

1 Adopt practices which are liberating and not guilt-inducing. Look for ways of prayer that make you want to intercede and give you positive encouragement that your prayer is worthwhile. This is not to say that prayer is for your satisfaction and enjoyment, rather that unless you feel positive about it, it will always be a struggle with failure.

2 Recognize the importance of the physical setting of prayer. Ascetism is not necessary in prayer. Indeed we pray much better when we have an environment where we are comfortable, relaxed but alert, surrounded by the things which help us to pray. These may be the Bible, a cross, an icon, a candle, a vase of flowers, a cassette player for music to help us settle into prayer. A prayer stool is helpful for many people. The important point is to have a regular place which your spirit recognizes as a place of prayer. Then you will quickly centre in and be ready to pray.

3 Take account of the relationship between personality and prayer. This is an area of spirituality being explored much more thoroughly these days, particularly through the insights of the Myers–Briggs Personality Type Indicator. Through this we can see that among the many other determinants of how we pray (family, early Christian experience, theology, culture) is the matter of our personality or temperament. Sometimes we may have wondered why we simply could not get on with a particular form of prayer which we were taught was normative, e.g., silence, praying with the Bible, charismatic prayer, formal liturgy, retreats, sacramental prayer, and so on. To know how our personality reacts with certain forms of prayer is not to narrow our options but to know where our home is, spiritually, so that we can confidently go out on journeys of the Spirit and enjoy all the territory God has given us. As we pray by ourselves, therefore, we may be able to let go of our shackles, find our home in a new way of praying and then enjoy our travels elsewhere.

4 Recognize that discipline is a vital part of any prayer.
No one is going to find that prayer is an undiluted and permanent
delight. Indeed the typical experience of prayer is that there is
much boredom, darkness and frustration. Distractions will
constantly attack us. Quiet, patient discipline is essential to the
process. The closer we are to something, the less we may actually
see it, and although we may not realize it at the time – because we
are too close to the detail – the value of our prayer time may have
been considerable. We simply have to stay in there.

**5 Intercession must be kept in balance with other forms
of prayer**. Intercession is only one part of the rich range of modes
of prayer. Giving God thanks, being aware of our failure, meditating
on Scripture and other nourishing books, looking into the glory of
God and being amazed – all these are forms of prayer which we
need to take into the crucible of our own spirituality, along with
intercession, and see where God the Holy Spirit leads us.

(64) GETTING STARTED

*If intercession is simply being with God with particular people and
situations on our heart, then personal prayer for others is ultimately very
straightforward. We just need to mention people and situations with a real
intention to hold them before God, not rushing through a list but naming
people in loving care. The more personal and genuine the language used, the
better, but sometimes it helps to have a simple phrase to use, such as the
following:*

> 'Lord, I am here before you, with *Kate* on my heart' . . . *silently
> hold Kate before God*
> 'Father, into the depths of your love I bring *Kate* . . . hold her
> and bless her . . .'
> 'Circle, Lord, your servant *Kate* with your healing love . . .'

*This simple naming of people or situations can be followed by further words
or by silence, as feels best to you. Words are not necessary, except that they*

may help us to focus our own thoughts and concern, and they may stop us racing on without due care and attention.

(65) THE TOUCH OF JESUS

If you find the use of your visual imagination helpful in prayer then the following approach may sometimes be useful. It has the merit of making the intercession very personal and of allowing you to linger over particular prayers. As so often in these less familiar approaches, initial strangeness need not put you off; it may simply be the novelty, and you may find that in time the style becomes very helpful.

As you pray, imagine that you are bringing the person you are praying for to meet Jesus. You may or may not be able to picture Jesus with clarity; there is no need to attempt that kind of detail. You bring your person to our Lord and step back out of the way. No words are needed, he knows the person's need quite well. Watch him gently lay hands on the person you have brought, in whatever way seems right. This may be a full embrace, a simple touch or a more formal laying on of hands on the head. Allow the exchange to go on as long as seems necessary and then watch as Christ lets the person go. There may be another person you then want to bring to him in the same way.

(66) PRAYER LISTS AND PRAYING HANDS

Many Christians keep long or short lists of people they want to pray for on a regular basis, or for a particular period. There are many different ways of ordering such lists. Some headings are often chosen, such as: family, friends, people in special need, Church and mission, social and global issues, etc. The problem is that the lists just grow and grow until they become unmanageable. How can you pray for so many people without it becoming a shopping list? And how can you start again without the seemingly violent act of cutting people out of your prayers?

Some practical suggestions

1 Make an initial decision about a maximum length for such prayer lists. This is your decision about what you can manage, and is the first step to getting on top of the problem. Be realistic rather than feel guilty. Make workable distinctions between short-term and long-term prayer commitments. If you can only function with reasonably short lists, accept that, and use one of the 'replacement strategies' below.

2 Organize your intercession list in such a way that different days belong to different groups of people and needs, except for the 'urgent–daily' category. It may be that there are certain groups who could be prayed for once a month, perhaps on the first of the month.

3 Limit yourself to a certain number of people for whom you will pray on any one day, and when you have finished, place the whole list – prayed and unprayed – in front of a cross or candle with a single prayer commending them all to God's care. I came by a pair of pottery hands, open in empty supplication, into which I place the list when I leave my time of prayer.

4 Don't be afraid to note when a particular need has been met, or substantial progress made, and to make a final prayer of thanks before crossing that person off the list with joy!

5 When the lists have got too long and a more radical step is needed, those lists can be held before God for the last time and then carefully burnt in a small bowl, while you pray that the needs of all these people and places will rise to God and be absorbed by him. It feels much better than throwing the lists in the waste-paper basket.

6 Use the major festivals, or the beginning of Lent and Advent, as automatic times of release, at which old lists can go with dignity and new ones be started.

CHRISTMAS CARDS, PHOTOGRAPHS AND DIARIES

It is often difficult to make intercession live, day by day, month by month. It is also difficult to know whether you are praying for a substantial range of people who share your life or for a narrow selection of more obvious people. The following ideas may help.

(67) CHRISTMAS CARDS

You can save the cards you received at Christmas and take five of them each day so that you can pray for the senders. You will be able to imagine their lives and needs, and will feel much more closely tied to them through the year. The relationship may strangely grow, and you might even be moved to phone them to show your interest and care more tangibly!

(68) PHOTOGRAPHS

It can be very useful to acquire photos of the people who you are pledged to pray for regularly, and to put them in an album. You can then pray for the people on one or two pages each day, with the extra vividness that comes from seeing the people in front of you. Remember to update the photos when you can, or you may find yourself praying in a time-warp!

(69) DIARIES AND CALENDARS

One way of praying for the realities of daily life is to take your diary into your time of prayer and to bring to God your own actions, meetings and commitments for the day or for the week. Moreover you can pray for those people whom you will be meeting, with all their needs, known to you and unknown. The open diary can itself speak powerfully of your desire to hold all of life open to God. Calendars are often rather unwieldy objects to take into prayer, but taking your calendar to God every month can be a good way of praying for the broader sweep of life's concerns, and it makes sure you are praying well in advance for important events. It may also be the place where birthdays are recorded and thus brought into your cycle of prayer.

(70) THE 'HOT DRINK OF LIGHT'

This is an idea commended by Angela Ashwin as a kind of 'first-aid' prayer for oneself, but it can be extended to prayer for others.

When you want to pray for someone in a concentrated way, visualize them being filled with light, as if a hot drink was being poured into them, and you were seeing them in a kind of X-ray. Pray that the light of Christ may flow into every part of their being, and see that prayer being answered. Pray that they will be warmed and healed by the love of Jesus Christ as he fills them with his peace, hope, joy – whatever the need is, and whatever the light therefore represents.

(71) LIVING WATER

John's Gospel is full of rich symbols which can be drawn into prayer. The following intercession depends on the person praying having the kind of imagination which can work with visualization. Otherwise, use another method. Jesus said: 'Whoever drinks the water that I give will never be thirsty again' (John 4.14). He promised 'living water', which would become a spring of life inside us.

Imagine the person you are praying for coming to the well . . . by the side of the well stands Jesus . . . see Jesus and your person in need, together . . . see the compassion and understanding in Jesus, his heart going out to your friend . . . see him take up a small jug and offer it to the other . . . see that person take the jug, drinking . . . and receiving living water, which brings healing, strength,

155

peace, the fullness of Christ's gift of himself . . . see any other exchange, word, conversation, gesture, between Jesus and the person prayed for . . . then see that person leave, refreshed, renewed.

(72) NEWSPAPERS

A common problem with prayer is that it operates at a level removed from the everyday world in which we live and make decisions, as if we are trying to keep our hands clean as we come to God. And yet it is the everyday world which God made and for which Christ died.

Every so often take a copy of the newspaper into your prayer time. Look at that front page and work your way around the main stories, taking each to God in focused, thoughtful prayer. The time is therefore spent partly in reading, partly in praying, and that's fine; life and prayer ought to be dovetailed in some such way, but beware the reading completely overtaking the praying. Some interesting questions arise: what do you pray for out of the sports pages? what is the relationship of God to fashion? Don't be afraid of not knowing how to pray: 'Lord, I'm confused. I don't know what to think about this. Help me to understand and not be dismissive. . . .' Over time we may begin to see the world more through God's eyes, and to be more sensitive to its complexity.

CIRCLING PRAYERS

Many people find it helpful to pray using the Celtic image of encircling people and situations in God's love. This enfolding or embracing corresponds to a deeply felt desire to care for those people, as a parent wraps up a child. The desire is therefore an authentic expression of prayer as a form of loving; but the enfolding here is actually God's, not ours; we leave the situation in God's embrace.

(73) CIRCLES

We can ask that the people we pray for should be encircled by that aspect of God's love which they seem to need. Few words are needed from us; we can let the silence lengthen as we place the person in God's care, and leave them there.

Circle Lord your servant *Anne* with your healing love . . .
Circle Lord your servant *Peter* with your protecting love . . .
Circle Lord your servant *Karen* with your consoling love . . .

By this method we are forced to think clearly about the heart of a person's need, to engage with some emotional effort in the act of prayer, and best of all to leave the outcome to God – not to give him a list of things to do.

(74) WIDENING CIRCLES

We can start this prayer with our immediate family or friends, seeing the circle of God's care and protection around these special people, and then widening the circle by stages so that more and more of God's world is brought into our prayer. At each stage particular people and needs will come to mind; these should be accepted and made the subject of prayer within that circle.

For example: 'Lord, place the circle of your love around our church family. Bless especially *Sue* and *George*, going through a difficult patch; and *Margaret* with her deep depression. Keep us all within

157

the circle of your peace, especially in that issue over the new hymnbook. . . .'

With each circle we might start: 'Lord, place the circle of your love around . . .' The circles might be: family, church family, neighbourhood, town or city, country, nations in special need, the earth. Finally the boundaries of our prayer are pushed back so that we are praying that God would 'reconcile all things to himself, whether things on earth or things in heaven' (Colossians 1.20). The concentration required of this form of prayer can be quite exhausting so we should know that it is not essential to go through the whole range of circles.

(75) THE 'JESUS BUBBLE'

I was moved and intrigued once to hear of a young girl in the parish who, when she prayed, took people into her 'Jesus bubble'. She simply imagined them within a bubble (a circle) with Jesus. She saw that the heart of prayer was being with Jesus. In terms of simplicity and clarity this innocent approach would be hard to beat.

ANYTIME PRAYER

Prayer often gets associated with particular times, such as a Sunday service, a morning 'quiet time', a daily office. Such special times of prayer are vital to a healthy life of prayer but that should not obscure the enormous value of having ways of praying through the day, so that the whole of our experience is tied to God. The opportunities for intercession are endless; here are some methods for 'anytime prayer'.

(76) TRIGGERS

We can use routine daily actions to trigger off a response of prayer for people in need. For example, when we turn on a tap and are waiting for the bowl to fill, we could pray for those who have to walk several miles every day to get clean water. Or when we are waiting in a supermarket checkout we could pray for those who have to spend much of their lives waiting – for someone to call, for a hospital appointment, for the end of a prison sentence. Or when we pick up a pen to start writing we could pause for a moment and pray for those millions all over the world who cannot write and are denied access to education. There are hundreds of other connections which could be made. It must not get obsessional, of course, or we might not get anything done all day!

(77) PRAYER ON THE STREETS

We often walk past people in the street and half notice someone with a disability or a stoop of the shoulders, or a person struggling with children or someone with a fearful look in their eyes. A hundred other signals are given out all the time by the details of people's body language (including ours). All of this can be turned into prayer. It means using our eyes actually to 'see' people rather than to look past them. An arrow prayer on their behalf costs us nothing, but gives God something to use. 'Lord, whatever it is that that man has to handle at the moment, give him grace to find the best way. Keep him and guard him. May he find you in the midst of it all.' Walking down the High Street becomes rather more interesting, in part because it makes us a lot more observant.

(78) CONKER PRAYERS

Some people find it helpful to have three conkers in their outdoor coat pocket, which they find whenever they sink their hands into it, and which remind them of the love and power of God the Trinity. As they walk along to work or take the dog out they might hold one conker and pray to God the Creator, in thanksgiving or concern for part of the created order. By taking hold of two conkers they might pray to Jesus Christ for his friendship and comfort for someone in need. As they take hold of three conkers they might pray to the Spirit for someone to be filled with all necessary courage or energy. Other objects can of course serve the same purpose – hazel nuts, marbles, or a single hand-shaped wooden cross.

FURTHER RESOURCES

It should be remembered that this book is specifically about intercession rather than the much broader subject of Christian prayer. There are many excellent books on prayer, therefore, which do not appear below because they lack the central focus of intercession.

General

These are useful collections of prayers for all sorts of situations.

George Appleton (ed.), *The Oxford Book of Prayer*. Oxford University Press 1985.
Angela Ashwin (ed.), *The Book of a Thousand Prayers*. Marshall Pickering 1996.
Mary Batchelor (ed.), *The Lion Prayer Collection*. Lion 1992.
Frank Colquhoun (ed.), *Parish Prayers*. Hodder & Stoughton 1967/1996.
Frank Colquhoun (ed.), *New Parish Prayers*. Hodder & Stoughton 1975/1996.
The SPCK Book of Christian Prayer. SPCK 1995.
Robert Van de Weyer, *The Fount Book of Prayer*. HarperCollins 1993.

Liturgical Collections

These give written-out examples of intercessions for a liturgical context, or material for services which includes some intercessory prayers.

Michael Counsell (ed.), *Prayers for Sundays*. HarperCollins 1994.
Michael Perham (ed.), *Enriching the Christian Year*. SPCK/Alcuin 1993.
Patterns for Worship. Church House Publishing 1995.
Susan Sayers, *Intercession for the Church's Year*. Kevin Mayhew 1991.

Special Interest

These books contain excellent material for particular situations, and contain many distinctive prayers.

Ian Cowie, *Prayers and Ideas for Healing Services.* Wild Goose Publications 1995.
Janet Morley (ed.), *Bread of Tomorrow. Praying With the World's Poor.* SPCK/Christian Aid 1992.
Janet Morley, *All Desires Known.* SPCK 1992.
Stephen Oliver (ed.), *Pastoral Prayers.* Mowbrays 1996.
Desmond Tutu, *An African Prayer Book.* Hodder & Stoughton 1995.
All Year Round. Churches Together in England. Three supplements each year.

All-age

These books contain much general material for all-age worship, and include some useful ideas for intercession.

Margaret Dean (ed.), *Pick and Mix.* Church House Publishing 1992.
Maggie Durran, *All-age Worship.* Angel Press 1987.
Peter Graystone and Eileen Turner, *A Church for All Ages.* Scripture Union 1993.
Dorothy Jamall, *Leaves on the Tree.* Church House Publications 1990.

Small Groups

The following books contain helpful material on intercession although they cover a wider territory of prayer.

Henry Morgan (ed.), *Approaches to Prayer.* SPCK 1991.
John Mallison, *Growing Christians in Small Groups.* Scripture Union 1989.
Michael Mitton, *Saints at Prayer.* Anglican Renewal Ministries 1994.

Personal Prayer

David Adam, *The Edge of Glory*. Triangle 1985.
David Adam, *Tides and Seasons*. Triangle 1989.
David Adam, *The Open Gate*. Triangle 1994.
Eddie Askew, *A Silence and a Shouting, Disguises of Love, Facing the Storm*, and Others. Leprosy Mission 1982, 1983, 1989.
Ruth Etchells, *Just As I Am*. Triangle 1994.
Giles and Melville Harcourt, *Short Prayers for the Long Day*. Collins 1987.
Margaret Pawley, *Praying for People*. Triangle 1990.
James Whitbourn, *A Prayer in the Life*. Triangle 1992.

Theology of intercession

These offer useful discussions of the complex issues surrounding prayer and God's providential activity in the world.

Tim Gorringe, *God's Theatre: A Theology of Providence*. SCM Press 1991.
John Polkinghorne, *Science and Providence*. SPCK 1989.
Vernon White, *The Fall of a Sparrow*. Paternoster 1985.

INDEX